THE UNIVERSITY OF MICHIGAN
CENTER FOR CHINESE STUDIES

MICHIGAN PAPERS IN CHINESE STUDIES
NO. 36

CHINESE DOMESTIC POLITICS AND
FOREIGN POLICY IN THE 1970s

by
Allen S. Whiting

Ann Arbor

Center for Chinese Studies
The University of Michigan

1979

Open access edition funded by the National Endowment for the Humanities/ Andrew W. Mellon Foundation Humanities Open Book Program.

Library of Congress Cataloging in Publication Data

Whiting, Allen Suess, 1926-
    Chinese domestic politics and foreign policy in the 1970s.

(Michigan papers in Chinese studies; no. 36)
    CONTENTS: Introduction.--PRC media images of the
U.S. and Taiwan, January-April 1976 and 1977.--Domestic
politics and foreign trade in the PRC, 1971-1976.
    1. China--Politics and government--1949-1976.
2. Mass media--Political aspects--China. I. Title.
II. Series.

DS777.55.W443   320.9'51'05   78-31865
ISBN 0-89264-036-7

Printed in the United States of America

ISBN 978-0-89264-036-2 (paper)
ISBN 978-0-472-12785-6 (ebook)
ISBN 978-0-472-90181-4 (open access)

CONTENTS

INTRODUCTION

These two studies explore the question of linkage between domestic politics in the People's Republic of China (PRC) and Peking's foreign policy.[1] This phenomenon has attracted much speculative attention abroad but it has rarely been examined empirically.[2] One reason is the general neglect of Chinese foreign policy as a subject of scholarly inquiry by comparison with the numerous works on internal politics.[3] Only a relatively few monographic studies have examined China's external behavior by utilizing original language materials to test hypotheses that permit comparison over time and that facilitate cumulative understanding.[4]

Much of the analytical problem, however, lies in the dearth of pertinent evidence. Although refugee interviews in Hong Kong throw considerable light on a wide range of domestic issues, they have proven to be of little use for research on foreign affairs.[5] The refugees are too far removed, physically and professionally, from the foreign policy process in Peking to have much interest in or information on the subject. The Chinese Nationalists on Taiwan, the United States government, and Hong Kong sources such as the Union Research Institute and the publication Ming-Pao have been invaluable in supplying PRC documents, including central directives and background briefing materials, on the Lin Piao affair and the "Gang of Four."[6] But the overwhelming bulk of this clandestinely acquired material concerns domestic politics, not foreign policy.[7] Perhaps the Peking leadership assumes that foreign policy is of relatively little concern for the majority of the population, except at such benchmark moments as the Kissinger-Nixon visits of 1971-72, which were given special attention in public and private commentaries.[8] In addition, foreign policy documents may be handled separately under special controls to minimize the possibility of their falling into the hands of other governments.[9]

Unfortunately, such materials on PRC foreign policy as have been disseminated from Taiwan do not stand up to close scrutiny as uniformly authentic and reliable.[10] Unlike their domestic policy counterparts,

1

which have proven valid both by scholarly examination and by subsequent revelations and publications from the mainland, these items appear to have been fabricated, in whole or in part. Such tampering has probably occurred before their arrival on Taiwan because these materials are carried on the classified index for use by official analysts doing secret studies. On occasion the documents contain references that run counter to presumed Chinese nationalist interests.[11] Whatever the source of contamination, however, those items distributed from Taiwan which purport to reveal PRC foreign policy as perceived or explained internally either do not pass the test of plausibility or bear telltale flaws in content.[12]

These circumstances limit but do not prevent the systematic examination of Peking's foreign policy, at least selected aspects thereof. One fruitful avenue of research lies in content analysis, quantitative and qualitative, of the media. [13] The two studies herein demonstrate the utility of this approach. In the first, conventional wisdom held that the "Gang of Four"--the radical faction headed by Chiang Ch'ing (Madame Mao Tse-tung)--opposed détente between the PRC and the U.S.[14] In view of the Gang's control of the media, the hypothesis arose that as between the faction's ascendancy in 1976 and its demise in 1977, the media would show a change in imagery dealing with the United States and with the Taiwan issue. On both matters this would move from negative to positive so far as the implications for détente were concerned. However, the opposite trend actually emerged in a rigorous comparison of People's Daily (Jen-min Jih-pao, hereafter JMJP) articles and monitored broadcasts for the period January-April of each year.

In the second study, the radicals' stress on "self-reliance" and the faction's nativistic emphasis in cultural affairs were widely assumed to underlay allegorical articles attacking the importation of whole plants and foreign technology. This assumption gained credence in detailed denunciation of the Gang's activities in this regard after its fall in October 1976. But this left unclear what effect such criticism had. On one hand, the actual contracts signed for major imports burgeoned from $58 million in 1972 to $1.2 billion in 1973 and then fell to $364 million in 1975 and $185 million in 1976.

On the other hand, a careful tracing of the ebb and flow as well as the content of press attacks against reliance on foreign technology between 1971 and 1976 showed no correlation with the timing of policy decision and implementation or any relevance to the economic pitfalls of the program. Instead, the media campaign began in 1974, after the program had peaked. It made no reference to the unanticipated problems associated with inflated import prices and shrinking export markets which resulted from the 1973 OPEC (Organization of Petroleum Exporting Countries) oil embargo and price increases. This suggested the determining factor to have been the state of politics in Peking and more specifically the physical state of Chou En-lai, rather than the economics of China's foreign trade.

Both studies show the danger of simplistic or impressionistic assumptions which link domestic politics with foreign policy. The lines of division between factions are not continuously drawn across all issue areas nor are they constant across time. Moreover, policy can be reactive to various stimuli, varying in the output according to context as well as to factional politics. These stimuli may be internal and stem from changes in the balance of power among individuals, factions, and coalitions, encouraging an attack or debate at one time and inhibiting it at another. They may also be external, wherein the march of events or probes by foreign sources invite or compel a response that otherwise might not occur.

Content analysis is more helpful for identifying the existence and range of debate than for explaining its cause or consequence. The editorial board of JMJP was changed twice between 1966 and 1977; the director of New China News Agency (Hsinhua, hereafter NCNA) was replaced twice. These developments suggest that some autonomy is given to such groups and individuals. At least they are held responsible post facto for the content of their organization's output. Precisely how much central control exists over Chinese media is unknown but presumably it too varies over time and across issue area.[15] Therefore, the existence of a line or divergencies therefrom must be placed in context to be properly evaluated for inferring top leadership perceptions, decisions, and goals.

Even when JMJP is directed from the center, it would be fallacious to assume that it accurately reflects leadership opinion. Foreign news may be deliberately distorted for several reasons. An external "enemy" may be exploited so as to spur domestic unity. It may be exaggerated as a threat in order to mobilize the masses for greater productivity. Foreign "friends" may be enlarged upon to instill confidence in China's international status. Insurgencies and "liberation movements" may be featured to heighten ideological credibility. A particular country may be shown in an uncritical light because its leadership is visiting Peking. In some instances, JMJP may be used as a medium of communication with foreign governments on the correct assumption that they analyze its contents for inferring PRC policy.

In addition to these various motivations for publishing material which may not correspond with the actual views of PRC decision makers, much information is withheld from the national media. Besides the omission of material at variance with the ideological tenets of Marxism-Leninism, three notable instances of foreign affairs reporting in crisis situations demonstrate the deliberate suppression of policy-relevant news in the media.[16] In September 1950, JMJP sharply reduced its coverage of the Korean War precisely when PRC concern over the intentions of General Douglas MacArthur provoked diplomatic efforts at deterring a United Nations entry into North Korea and military deployments began prior to Chinese intervention. In the spring of 1962, no information appeared in JMJP reflecting apprehension over perceived indicators of a Chinese nationalist intent to invade the mainland after three years of PRC economic disorders. However, on 23 June, NCNA offered a detailed recapitulation of these indicators, immediately after a diplomatic demarche was made to the United States through an ambassadorial meeting at Warsaw. Again in the summer of 1962, Chinese media carried nothing to reveal tension with the Soviet Union over the border province of Sinkiang. Yet, Peking subsequently officially charged Moscow with trying to "detach" the area by encouraging a mass exodus of non-Chinese peoples and inciting riots in a major city.

These examples caution against equating JMJP images with official perceptions. As a routine consideration, the practical constraints of limited space make selectivity and suppression inevitable. But to the extent that this takes on regularity in thematic content, either through inclusion or exclusion, it bears analysis of intent.

We are sensitive to these various problems in utilizing the Chinese press. However, the positive aspects of content analysis deserve attention. JMJP is primarily a domestic medium of communication. While it also serves as a source for foreign observers in Peking and abroad, the newspaper's main audience is internal. True, on rare occasion an instance of "signalling" may manipulate its content for a specific foreign target. For example, JMJP strengthened deterrence signals to India during the 1962 border confrontation by increased front page and editorial attention to the issue.[17] Such an instance, however, is the exception and not the rule. In the examples of suppression noted above, JMJP silence actually obscured the "signal" for perceived enemies abroad. Suppression occurred because of the presumed negative effect that publication would have on the Chinese audience whose sense of external threat is substantially derived from JMJP.

Therefore, JMJP should not be regarded as primarily designed to influence foreign governments. Rather, it can be taken as a domestic communications channel between the government or an important sector thereof and key publics in the PRC. To a significant degree the images it projects are those officially held by the Chinese body politic.

How much these images correspond to privately held views of the highest level can only be surmised. We know from authoritative versions of Mao's previously unpublished statements that during the 1950s he explicitly disparaged the threat potential of "U.S. imperialism" in flat contradiction of PRC propaganda.[18] Similarly, Mao pursued the prospects of a Nixon visit in 1970-71 while PRC media operated at full strength castigating "U.S. imperialism and its running dogs" over the Indochina war. Thus, neither total congruence nor total contradiction can be assumed a priori as between publicly conveyed images and actual policy.

Radio monitoring was used sparingly in these studies. All issues of a newspaper or journal can be compared in toto over time for the size, location, and content of various items, and headlines can be compared in size and content, but radio monitor reports only provide selected contents in translation. They offer no way of determining an item's position in a particular program, the frequency of repetition, or the nuance of delivery.[19]

One research strategy deserves favorable attention. NCNA daily reports in English, distributed in London, contain numerous foreign press stories and original NCNA items on international affairs, some of which do not appear in JMJP. Comparison of inclusion and exclusion reveals patterns which suggest deliberate choice and editorial policy according to thematic content and timing.[20]

A separate study, not included herein, illustrated the utility of combining attention to the NCNA-JMJP relationship with headline analysis.[21] For the period 1 January-30 September 1977, all JMJP and Foreign Broadcast Information Service (FBIS) material pertinent to the Korean problem was examined and compared with statements emanating from the Democratic People's Republic of Korea (DPRK). Peking's public reaction to the announcement by President Carter of a unilateral withdrawal of U.S. forces from South Korea substantively paralleled that of Pyongyang. The withdrawal was termed "a gesture" in response to "the firm opposition of the entire Korean people and the pressure of public opinion at home and abroad."[22] The U.S. was accused of

intending to remain in the South "to obstruct the Korean people's independent and peaceful reunification . . . and create 'two Koreas' so as
to perpetuate the division of Korea." Peking also stepped up its demand
for "the complete withdrawal of all U.S. forces" by adding the word
"immediate" before "complete," in line with Pyongyang's official response to the Carter announcement.

Closer examination showed, however, that the PRC position
remained somewhat behind and removed from that of the DPRK.
Pyongyang's statements appeared selectively in JMJP or not at all.
NCNA usually reprinted North Korean releases belatedly and even
longer delays marked their appearance in JMJP. The more strident
their anti-American tone, the more likely they were to be specifically
identified as of Korean source in the headline. None of Pyongyang's
accusations linking the U.S. military presence with Japan appeared
in JMJP.

Thus, a simple reading of selected statements would suggest a
virtual identity of posture between Peking and Pyongyang during this
period. But content analysis reveals significant delays and differences
of emphasis in Chinese media compared with that of North Korea.
Further exploration of the relationship between NCNA releases and
JMJP coverage should prove useful in determining the way images of
the external world are deliberately shaped for domestic consumption.

The accompanying analysis of politics and foreign trade illustrates
the need to relate media material with actual behavior. This approach
required taking into account the delay between the decision to import
an item and the final conclusion of a contract, during which time extensive investigation and prolonged negotiation may occur.[23] Information
is often lacking on some of these intervening steps. But without some
such reconstruction of development, it is impossible to determine
whether an apparent debate is aimed at a prospective policy or is
retrospectively targetting those who advocated and implemented either
past or existing policy.

In sum, these two studies were designed to be of interest for
their methodology as well as their substance. While they focus on
specific topics in a fixed time period with well-known outcomes, their
policy implications will remain relevant in the near future. Hopefully
analytic utility will outlast their manifest content.

PRC Media Images of the U.S. and Taiwan
January-April 1976 and 1977

Project Design

This study tested for linkages between domestic politics and foreign policy in the PRC during the first four months of 1976 and 1977.
It focuses on images of the United States, the U.S.-Soviet relationship,
and Taiwan presented in JMJP as the main medium for printed news in
China. In addition, monitored Chinese broadcasts as selectively available in translation through FBIS were examined for an authoritative but
less comprehensive source.

The initial hypothesis held that the Gang of Four--Chiang Ch'ing,
Chang Ch'un-ch'iao, Wang Hung-wen, and Yao Wen-yuan--manipulated
the media to denigrate détente with the United States. This hypothesis
and its corollary, namely, that images favorable to Sino-American
détente improved with the Gang's downfall, reflected conventional
wisdom and intuitive impressions held by foreign observers in 1976. [1]
It also reflected Chinese intimations made after the purge of Chiang
Ch'ing and her cohorts. [2] Moreover, according to a reliable French
report, the assistant editor-in-chief of JMJP claimed that his newspaper
was Yao Wen-yuan's "fief" which "spread lies" under his direction. [3]

The motivation of the Gang in denigrating détente with the U.S. was
presumed to have been both personal, to attack Chou En-lai as its most
public practitioner, and ideological, to emphasize the struggle against
"U.S. imperialism." Evidence of this would be most apparent during
the period January-April 1976, after Chou's death removed all need
for constraint. Conversely, a more favorable treatment of the images
and issues associated with Sino-American détente would be expected in
January-April 1977 after the Gang had fallen.

As a secondary goal, various approaches were utilized to test
alternative methodologies. Systematic measures for quantitative

analysis of <u>JMJP</u> utilized the length and location of news items together with thematic content to permit discrete comparisons over time. Comparison of NCNA releases in English with those appearing in <u>JMJP</u> offered another dimension of media behavior with suggestive relevance.

In addition to news stories, analytical inferences were drawn from <u>JMJP</u> headlines. Headlines in Chinese communist newspapers appear to be deliberately calculated according to political considerations rather than determined by last-minute considerations of space count and visual layout desiderata as in the conventional capitalist press. Specific instructions on type size, page positioning, and line count are transmitted daily from central to provincial newspapers, as occasionally reprinted in <u>FBIS</u>. A western scholar visiting Shanghai in October 1976 after the Gang of Four was overthrown saw a wall-poster which juxtaposed that day's front page from <u>JMJP</u> and Shanghai's <u>Wen-hui Pao</u>, highlighting subtle differences in political content which were obscured by the apparent identity of composition.[4]

An earlier study showed headlines to correlate with changes of policy and "signals" in the Sino-Indian border crisis of 1962.[5] Similarly, the comparison of <u>JMJP</u> headlines during January-April 1976 and January-April 1977 revealed patterns of consistency and change, the implications of which become evident when placed against the overall data. A fuller exposition of the coding procedures is appended at the end of this study together with a complete presentation of the thematic breakdown and statistical data. Only summary tables are included in the main text. Radio broadcasts provided a rough basis for comparison with <u>JMJP</u> so far as the treatment of particular subject matter is concerned. Finally, qualitative analysis focused on statements of unique importance or salience in the Chinese media. As an adjunct, two books published in 1977 by a left-wing firm in Hong Kong also proved pertinent.

Aggregate Analysis of U.S. Articles

A total of 412 items relating to the United States in <u>JMJP</u> of January-April 1976 and 1977 were analyzed for their portrayal of American domestic and foreign policy developments in terms of favorable versus unfavorable content (see table 1; for full details see Appendix A, B). Approximately half showed a clear bias in 1976 but only one-third could be so coded in 1977. The somewhat greater emphasis given to unfavorable stories declined slightly, 4.3 percent as against 2 percent being the differential for 1976 and 1977.

TABLE 1

U.S. NEWS ITEMS IN JMJP
1 JANUARY TO 30 APRIL 1976 AND 1977

	1976		1977	
	No. of Items	Percentage	No. of Items	Percentage
Favorable	49	23.2	31	15.4
Unfavorable	58	27.5	35	17.4
Others	104	49.3	135	67.2
Total	211	100.0	201	100.0

On United States foreign policy per se, comparison of March 1977 NCNA English language news releases with those printed in JMJP showed a much greater printing of favorable (63 percent) than unfavorable (23 percent) items. Five of the six stories on Latin America that were anti-U.S. never appeared in JMJP, including three on the Panama Canal and one that reported the termination by Brazil of American military assistance. The sixth, also on the Canal Zone, was delayed fifteen days between the NCNA releases and JMJP printing. In April 1977 two additional stories on Panama appeared in JMJP nine and fifteen days after their NCNA release. All such stories won little space.

This pattern of downplaying U.S. weakness in its immediate sphere of influence could reflect a desire to keep open the credible use of American power to offset the Soviet Union. This hypothesis is strengthened by examination of unfavorable stories concerning U.S. foreign relations appearing in JMJP (see table 2). These had headlines that generally omitted reference to the U.S. or were smaller in type size as compared with other headlines on the same page. This is particularly evident in 1977 where all such stories were so treated whereas in 1976 one-third of the U.S.-associated headlines exceeded average type size. They also tended to be of shorter than average length, with only one exceeding thirty-five square inches in 1977 as against ten, or one-third, in 1976. Finally, the majority of such 1976 items were related to Korea and Cambodia; in 1977 only one concerned China directly.

TABLE 2

UNFAVORABLE STORIES ON U.S. FOREIGN POLICY
1 JANUARY TO 30 APRIL 1976 AND 1977

	1976	1977
Headline Size and Content		
U.S. not specified	13	7
U.S. line 6th largest on page or less	6	4
U.S. line 1st to 5th largest on page	10	--
Space		
35 sq. in. or less	19	10
36–55 sq. in.	5	--
56–65 sq. in.	1	1
above 66 sq. in.	4	--

Because this study focused explicitly on images of the United States and only included the Soviet Union as a function thereof, sufficient data is not available for a precise comparison of how the two countries are treated in their various dimensions. In general, however, unfavorable accounts of Soviet external relations exceeded those on the United States in all of the above categories of measurement. As in the relative

treatment of both superpowers in single speeches and articles, the
U.S.S.R. received the greater emphasis in the level of attention, space,
and frequency of reference. Although in 1977 the two superpowers
tended to be specifically identified by name while in 1976 such explicit-
ness was usually reserved for Moscow, this did not indicate a PRC
policy of equidistance. There is no question but that the United States
remained the lesser of two evils.

U.S.-U.S.S.R. Relationship

A total of 304 stories associated with the U.S.-U.S.S.R. relationship appeared in JMJP during the periods under examination (see table 3).

TABLE 3

ITEMS ON U.S.-U.S.S.R. RELATIONS IN JMJP
1 JANUARY TO 30 APRIL 1976 AND 1977

	1976		1977	
	No. of Items	%	No. of Items	%
U.S./U.S.S.R. Bilateral Relations	94	61.1	107	71.4
U.S./U.S.S.R./Third World Relations	60	38.9	43	28.6
	154	100.0	150	100.0

While the total is roughly the same for 1976 and 1977, greater attention
was accorded bilateral aspects in 1977 than in 1976 (71.4 percent as
against 61.1 percent).

A striking change in the images associated with Soviet-American
relations in 1977 as compared with 1976 showed the power of Moscow
on the ascendant while that of Washington was on the wane. However,
a reversal in this trend was implicitly possible because American
public opinion was shown as increasingly opposed to Soviet behavior.

Specifically, headlines portraying both superpowers in diplomatic or verbal contention, or in a conventional or nuclear arms race, doubled (7-15) from 1976 to 1977 (for full details see Appendix D). Those that showed the U.S.S.R. challenging U.S. security, vital interests, or spheres of influence, also doubled (3-6). The Carter administration initiatives on SALT and their rebuff by Moscow accounted for an extraordinary increase (1-16) in stories which alleged that neither side was genuinely committed to détente and arms limitation.

Items that portray the Soviet Union as achieving or aiming at strategic superiority over the U.S. quadrupled (2-8). Conversely, depiction of the American defense capability as moving to offset the U.S.S.R.'s greater strength nearly disappeared (5-1). The Soviet Union was increasingly shown as exploiting détente for military buildup and expansion (1-5), facilitated by economic assistance from the U.S. and Western Europe (1-6).

The internal consistency of these themes which emerged from more than three hundred articles concerning the U.S.-U.S.S.R. relationship, together with the sharp numerical disparities as between 1976 and 1977, reveals a coherent policy of presentation. To what extent this policy represents the actual assessment held within the PRC leadership is impossible to say. However, the credibility of the presentation is documented in a Chinese translation, published in Hong Kong, of the Drew Middleton book Can America Win the Next War? (New York: Charles Scribner's Sons, 1975, 271pp.). While not directly comparable with official PRC media material, the volume deserves consideration at this point.

This translation appeared in March 1977 under the imprimatur of a left-wing publisher, Ch'i Shih Nien Tai Yueh K'an. Although not an explicitly communist organization nor under known direction from Peking, this organization has nonetheless supported PRC policy positions. The investment of money and effort in book translation, the marginal commercial prospects for such a volume among overseas Chinese audiences, and the political sensitivity of the subject matter all suggest that this was sponsored at higher levels. Such sponsorship was implied by the prominence given the book by China Arts and Crafts, the official PRC outlet. At its main Kowloon store, the book was featured on a table together with the fifth volume of Mao's Selected Works and two volumes of tribute to the late Chou En-lai.

Middleton provides an authoritative, detailed analysis of weapons postures--Soviet, NATO, and American--together with political developments which prompt him to answer his provocative title, "probably not." The "next war" is explicitly limited to Europe and is foreseen as conventional, not nuclear. This corresponds with views expressed privately by high Chinese officials in 1975 who gave the same scenario as justification for their public forecast that "a third world war is inevitable."[6] Middleton's conclusions spell out the implications of JMJP images concerning the U.S.-Soviet power balance:

> Under military, political, and social conditions in
> the United States and among our chief allies of
> today and the next three or four years, the West,
> meaning NATO, could not win a conventional war
> in Europe in the sense that the Soviet forces would
> be halted short of their primary objectives and
> eventually driven back to Eastern Europe. . . . (p. 252)

> The fighting is likely to end with the Russians
> ruling most of Western Europe and the Americans,
> perhaps with Britain as an outpost, perhaps not,
> concentrating on a Fortress America on which the
> next phase in the duel will be based. . . . Resumption of the war will require not only an explosion
> of patriotism on the part of the public but a national
> effort beyond anything the United States has ever
> known. (p. 259)

JMJP did not exclude the possibility that "the public" may indeed turn U.S. military policy around. On the contrary, stories indicating opposition in American public opinion to Soviet behavior and strength increased sharply from 1976 to 1977 (1-9). This contrasts with images of declining West European public resistance to the Soviet Union (13-7), perhaps reflecting the greater communist strength in France and Italy. Thus, the treatment left the prospects for future American military policy somewhat open, although specific trend analysis was weighted on the side of pessimism.

Consistent with the foregoing, JMJP sharply decreased its presentation of convergent Soviet and American interests (4-1). This implies a greater possibility of exploiting superpower contention to China's advantage. However, the utility of relying on the U.S. to offset the U.S.S.R. was brought into question by the overall trend in the military, economic, and political factors that affect the strategic balance. In sum, while the Soviet Union remained the greater threat, the United States became a lesser pseudoally.

It is important to note the paucity of substantive comment, signed articles, and JMJP editorials on the Soviet-American relationship. The overwhelming majority of items dealing with this topic are NCNA releases derived from foreign press reports. As such, the themes received far less attention than did the alleged iniquities of "Soviet social imperialism" which were treated in extensive detail and featured prominently in signed articles and special commentaries.

Sino-U.S. Relations and Taiwan

Sino-American relations are rarely the subject of direct or extensive treatment in JMJP. Items in this regard were greater in 1976 than 1977 in terms of frequency, size, and favorable content because of material related to the visits of Julie and David Eisenhower and former president Richard Nixon (see Appendix C). However, one major exception occurred in a unique article which recapitulated Chou En-lai's role in foreign policy on the first anniversary of his death.[7] Given one and a half pages in JMJP, the article was reprinted in Peking Review in a slightly truncated version. The authorship, "Theory Study Group of the Ministry of Foreign Affairs," attested to its authenticity.

In this article, unfavorable references to "U.S. imperialism" occupied nearly twice the space given to favorable references. Nearly 40 percent of the negative material concerned the Indochina War with another 30 percent on the Korean War. Positive attention focused exclusively on the Sino-American ambassadorial exchanges following the 1955 Bandung Conference and the 1971-72 developments up to and including President Nixon's first visit to the PRC. Significantly, the space given to unfavorable treatment of the U.S.S.R. is virtually identical with that for the United States.

The slant of this article is surprising in view of the prominent role that Chou played in promoting détente and personally receiving American visitors in 1971-74. The Peking Review version omitted the observation, "After the victory of the War of Resistance Against Japan, in the name of mediation, U.S. imperialism supported and instigated Chiang Kai-shek to start an all-out civil war. . . . Premier Chou . . . waged an acute, complicated, and tit-for-tat

struggle against U.S. imperialism and its running dogs."[8] Pointed
reference was made to Chou's going to Bandung for the First Afro-
Asian Conference "although . . . there was a grave threat to his
safety just after U.S.-Chiang secret agents had engineered the
blowing up of the airliner Kashmir Princess."[9] Peking Review added
a footnote to explain the explosion which killed all eleven of the Chinese
and Vietnamese staff members on board, "This incident was created
by U.S.-Chiang secret agents who planned to assassinate the members
of the delegation headed by Premier Chou so as to sabotage the conference."[10]

So far as salience and significance are concerned, this essay was
the most important statement on Chinese foreign policy in general and
Sino-American relations in particular to appear during the period
January-April 1977.[11] It countered the moderate tone of JMJP by
showing "U.S. imperialism" in a much harsher light, recalling times
of confrontation such as the 1958 Quemoy-Matsu imbroglio and the
Kashmir Princess incident that are normally omitted from such
accounts. The treatment of Taiwan was unique in several respects.
Taiwan concerned Chou "even when [he was] seriously ill." It was his
"initiative that led to the subsequent Sino-U.S. ambassadorial talks"
following the Bandung conference. "On different occasions and in
different ways, Premier Chou sternly denounced U.S. imperialist
aggression" on Taiwan.

Chou's position was summarized as follows: "The Chinese people
are determined to liberate Taiwan, and this is China's internal affair
which brooks no foreign interference." The last portion of this statement had not appeared in PRC media in this formulation for five years
but subsequent to this article it was prominently featured.[12] The
next paragraph returned to a basic PRC position of the mid-1950s that
had not been given publicly for at least a decade:

> The Chinese Government's principled stand on the
> liberation of Taiwan which is China's internal affair
> is firm and unshakable. But regarding the dispute
> between China and the United States resulting from
> the forcible U.S. occupation of Taiwan, the Chinese
> Government has always stood for a settlement through
> negotiations without resorting to force.[13]

An important distinction was drawn between the question of Taiwan
per se and ending "the forcible U.S. occupation of Taiwan" through
"negotiations without resorting to force." This carried obvious implications in view of the persistent United States expression of "interest

in the peaceful resolution of the Taiwan problem" and the continued
American security guarantee to the Republic of China.

This article set the general tone of the PRC media's treatment of
Taiwan, which underwent significant changes between 1976 and 1977.
JMJP coverage expanded from 998 to 1,226 square inches, including
photographs (see table 4).

TABLE 4

SPACE AND LOCATION OF JMJP COVERAGE ON TAIWAN
1 JANUARY TO 30 APRIL 1976 AND 1977
(in square inches)

	p. 1	p. 2	p. 3	p. 4	p. 5	Photo	Total
All Stories on Taiwan							
1976			227	498	248	25	998
1977	92	526	69	293	178	155	1266
All Stories on Taiwan except those on or about 28 February							
1976			162	378	0	0	540
1977			69	218	144	0	431

More striking is the fact that no Taiwan material appeared on page one
or two in 1976 whereas these pages carried 92 and 526 square inches
respectively in 1977.

This increased JMJP attention was largely associated with the
thirtieth anniversary of "2-28," the 28 February 1947 incident which
began as a small riot in Taipei and expanded into a pogrom by the
Chinese Nationalist military against the Taiwanese political and
intellectual elite. Foreign estimates claimed that up to ten thousand
Taiwanese died in the subsequent month of terror. Many fled to Japan.
The incident is traditionally treated in PRC media as a deliberate
uprising, allegedly coordinated with the communist offensive on the
mainland. Because decentennials are especially featured in Chinese

commemoration, this evoked a greater celebration in 1977 than 1976. The ceremonies in Peking reportedly drew three hundred as compared with the previous one hundred persons and had three Politburo members present instead of one.

These considerations, however, do not account for the thematic changes from 1976 to 1977 (see Appendix F). On one hand, articles and broadcasts on Taiwan's internal situation which made no reference to liberation prospects or Chinese determination related thereto were fewer in 1977 or showed no change of frequency. An equal number in 1976 and 1977 merely expressed the wish for or belief in Taiwan's liberation. On the other hand, those items which pledged a mainland contribution to liberation were up sharply (3-13) in 1977. More significantly, those which expressed a sense of urgency by the phrase "early liberation" (emphasis added) increased from 1 to 9 between 1976 and 1977, suggesting a deliberate change in the line.

No detailed scenario was given and the regime did not commit itself to any particular timetable of course of action. A slight hint emerged with respect to the possible need to use force, wholly absent in 1976 but occurring on three instances in 1977. However, as shown in the appendix, these are oblique and nonauthoritative.

In addition, a special postage stamp was issued to commemorate "2-28" with the slogan, "We are determined to liberate Taiwan." On 1 March, Chairman Hua Kuo-feng replaced Mao with a quotation in the conventional upper right-hand corner box on page one of JMJP, "We are determined to accomplish the sacred task of completely liberating Taiwan and unifying the fatherland."

Although considerably less authoritative, a suggestive source of images associated with the Taiwan issue is an unusual volume, also published in March 1977 by the aforementioned Hong Kong firm.[14] A documentary compilation on Sino-American relations, 1940-76, this book encompasses more than one hundred items in 380 pages, followed by a 56-page chronology covering selected events from 1784 to 1976. It includes full translations of speeches and press conferences by American officials, excerpts from congressional reports, and similar materials not normally available to Chinese readers.

The volume offers no analysis or commentary. However, a brief introduction dated January 1977 apologizes, inter alia, for including material attributed to such fallen figures as P'eng Teh-huai and Ch'iao

Kuan-hua. Because they did not speak "as individuals" but as government officials, inclusion of their statements was necessary "to understand" such events as the 1958 Quemoy episode and PRC entry into the United Nations.

The chronology is illuminating in its treatment of the period 1973-76 which covers fourteen pages. Visits by American officials to Taiwan are meticulously recorded. Reference is made to the Republic of China's (ROC) alleged effort to produce an atomic bomb. Developments which bear no special date, such as the additional four consulates granted to the ROC and Northrop Aviation's assistance in building the F5-E fighter factory, are omitted here but can be found in the documentary material.

Excluding those items which neither help nor hinder better relations between the PRC and the U.S., the balance of positive versus negative references shifts markedly over time: in 1973, 18 to 9; 1974, 10 to 35; and 1975, 6 to 33. The trend breaks with 1976, where only six events are entered on each side of the ledger. Omitted from the 1976 tabulation were statements which emerged in the American presidential campaign, such as the platform positions of both parties and remarks on Taiwan by the various candidates. These omissions presumably were deliberate. Perhaps in parallel with the open-ended implications of JMJP materials dealing with the U.S.-U.S.S.R. relationship, it was deemed prudent to avoid prejudging the new administration on this matter.

The timing and content of this compilation require comment. No particular event, positive or negative, explains the publication of this documentary collection in 1977. This was not a watershed year in Sino-American relations as were 1950 and 1972. Moreover, the pattern of emphasis in the choice of documents and developments chronicled at considerable length reflects unfavorably on Sino-American détente. For example, the PRC entry into the United Nations in October 1971 occurs after twenty pages of quotation from press conferences and statements by Secretary of State William Rogers and Ambassador to the U.N. George Bush, all strongly opposing expulsion of the ROC. The PRC entry is marked by Ambassador Ch'iao Kuan-hua's initial speech and a victorious JMJP editorial, both of which attack the U.S. position. The 1958 Quemoy confrontation covers forty pages of material, including sharply hostile remarks by then Vice-President Richard Nixon. Numerous protests from the Ministry of Foreign Affairs together with NCNA reports concerning American bombing on North Vietnam and alleged attacks on Chinese shipping are also quoted.

Taken in conjunction with the shift in emphasis and attention given to the Taiwan issue by PRC media, the book appears to reflect a summing-up of Sino-American détente wherein the balance on this particular count is found wanting from a PRC perspective. The American tie to Taiwan is shown not to have dissolved with détente. On the contrary, it actually strengthened, at least on the political and economic dimensions represented in the documents and chronology. While the withdrawal of American military personnel from Quemoy and Matsu in 1976 is noted, as is the earlier removal of the F-4 squadrons, the systematic drawdown of Washington's military presence is ignored. Loans from the Export-Import Bank to the ROC are itemized. Statements by congressmen favoring full normalization receive attention but so do ROC protests against American presidential visits to the mainland. The conflicting images of the relationship are most sharply juxtaposed when the Ministry of Foreign Affairs statement of 26 November 1968, which for the first time formally and publicly proposed a Sino-American agreement on the Five Principles of Peaceful Coexistence, is followed immediately by Mao Tse-tung's celebrated call of 20 May 1970 for the overthrow of "U.S. imperialism and all its running dogs."

As in other materials, the book stops short of a "worst case" portrayal of the U.S.-Taiwan linkage. We have already noted the omission of 1976 campaign statements which reaffirmed the American security interest. In addition, the documentary collection and the chronology omit all reference to the June 1962 crisis wherein the PRC publicly accused the United States of helping Chiang Kai-shek prepare for an imminent invasion. Conversely, every American visit to Peking of possibly favorable import is included, as is former Secretary of Defense James Schlesinger's trip of September 1976.

The same caveat applies to this volume as to the Middleton translation; that is, it is not expressly issued by a PRC publisher. It is in nonsimplified Chinese type, designed for an overseas and not a mainland audience. However, the same positive inference also applies: the circumstances of publication argue for the book as having been authorized by PRC officials. Its prominent display in Hong Kong communist bookstores further supports this inference.

One final addendum on Taiwan must be noted. FBIS monitoring of broadcasts focused on Taiwan showed a 50 percent decrease in externally directed programs between January-April of 1976 and 1977 while the number of domestic programs remained constant (see Appendix G). The drop occurred in Mandarin broadcasts to Taiwan:

five to one from Fukien and nine to none from Peking Radio. However, Peking's programs in English increased slightly from eight to ten.

This reversal of the JMJP increase in the frequency of Taiwan items and the decline in Mandarin broadcasts to Taiwan may be explained by the general change in thematic content. Whereas in 1976 considerable emphasis was given to internal Taiwan conditions and the prospect of liberation by the Taiwanese themselves, these themes faded or disappeared completely in 1977 broadcasts.. This change paralleled the JMJP shift to greater emphasis on the mainland's role in liberation and correspondingly less on that of the island's population.

Whereas several dimensions of measurement are possible with JMJP, only a rough frequency count and thematic analysis can be done with FBIS. Inferences must remain tentative in the absence of total program content. Without knowledge of the daily broadcast schedule, the location of items in a particular program, and their frequency of rebroadcast, it is hazardous to speculate further on changes from 1976 to 1977. However, congruence on key points between JMJP and FBIS strengthens analysis based solely on the press.

Findings and Observations

1. This research revealed the following patterns of consistency and change in the treatment of selected issues by PRC media during January-April 1976 compared with the same period in 1977:

    a) unfavorable images of the U.S. prevailed over favorable in both years;

    b) somewhat less emphasis was given to unfavorable images of the U.S. in 1977 than in 1976;

    c) this positive shift was particularly evident with respect to U.S. policy in terms of headlines, space, and frequency;

    d) a markedly negative shift occurred from 1976 to 1977 in the depiction of the U.S.-U.S.S.R. power relationship with the U.S. shown as weakening and the U.S.S.R. as strengthening;

    e) the Taiwan issue was more prominently featured in 1977 than in 1976;

    f) the thematic content of Taiwan materials in 1977 strengthened the mainland's role in "liberation" compared with that of the population on Taiwan, added references to the possible use of force, and alluded to the desired "early" nature of the goal.

2. The relevant data negates the initial hypothesis that the Gang of Four manipulated the major media so as to denigrate Sino-American détente. The major PRC goal in détente was to balance U.S. power against the U.S.S.R. threat. Yet media themes pertinent to this balance showed the U.S. to better advantage in 1976 when Chiang Ch'ing and her cohorts were up than in 1977 when they were down. In addition, the most sensitive issue in PRC-U.S. relations—Taiwan—was muted in the immediate post-Chou period compared with its greater prominence and more assertive treatment in 1977.

This finding is consistent with the failure of attacks on the Gang to accuse them of any specific misdeeds with respect to Sino-American relations. In one instance, however, they were accused of compromise on the Taiwan issue. Specifically, a Taiwan sports group alleged that the Gang had

schemed to obstruct the struggle to liberate Taiwan, interfering with the strategic planning of Chairman Mao, deliberately opposing the relevant directives of Premier Chou. The old capitulationist, dog-headed councillor Chang Ch'un-ch'iao, using the power he usurped, openly opposed publicizing to Taiwan the renowned statement of Chairman Mao, "WITHOUT THE BROOM, THE DUST AS A RULE WILL NOT DISAPPEAR BY ITSELF." He forbade the use of the word "condemn" in an article retorting the Chiang gang's slander and rumor-making. [15]

3. A bureaucratic politics hypothesis would argue that the change in images of the U.S.-U.S.S.R. power balance and the stress on "liberation of Taiwan" represent manipulation of the media by military interests which seek greater appropriations for modern weaponry. This hypothesis cannot be disproven within the limits of this research. The public attention given to an apparent debate over weapons and strategy in the spring of 1977 was without precedent in the PRC press. A systematic examination of that material and its differing lines of argument in correlation with the data presented above might permit more confident conclusions to be drawn.

At this point, however, the evidence is neither solid nor sufficient to support bureaucratic politics as a central explanation. This approach assumes a greater control over JMJP by military interests than can be inferred from its past operation and present editorial staff. The People's Liberation Army (PLA) traditionally employs Liberation Daily (Chieh-fang-chün Pao) as its medium of communication, entering JMJP mainly through joint editorials and special commentaries or speeches. Moreover, it has no known connection with the Hong Kong publishing house which translated the Drew Middleton volume, Can America Win the Next War?

On balance, it seems more likely that the debate over military weapons and defense in the spring of 1977 was not related to the change in imagery on U.S.-Soviet relations and Taiwan.

4. A more sophisticated hypothesis links bureaucratic and domestic politics to posit coalitions between governmental interest groups and political factions as determining foreign policy output.[16] In this context the priority given by the Gang of Four to ideological as opposed to practical matters, whether economic or military, tended to suppress discussion of power balance, strategy, and weapons. Their domination of the media therefore presented a set of concerns at considerable variance with those held elsewhere within the government, particularly among military and developmental interests, as well as by their opponents in the Party such as Teng Hsiao-p'ing. Their overthrow by a coalition of interests wherein economic and military rationality prevailed permitted a different focus in JMJP, manifest in the shifts of thematic content and emphasis noted above.

A fuller explication and testing of this hypothesis would go well beyond the limits of this study. It is compatible with a general sense of Chinese politics emergent in recent academic and governmental analyses. It fits the main lines of media content as conventionally understood over the last two years. Missing from most such analysis, however, is the explicit identification of individuals, groups, and interests that comprise competing coalitions and evidence on their composition over time and across issue areas.

This hypothesis does not exclude an explanation which attributes changing imagery to changing policy assessment. This change could emerge within the same coalition or through replacement of one coalition by another. While the cause is different, the consequence is the same: a change in policy resulting in a change in media images.

5. Another hypothesis holds that media manipulation on the Taiwan question is separate in design from that on Soviet-American relations and is directed toward anticipated negotiations. Under this explanation a harder Taiwan line is the logical bargaining position to be staked out in advance. Two objections arise, however. First and most fundamental is the implausibility of resorting to such a subtle, indirect, and complicated means of "signalling" when more unambiguous, direct channels exist and are utilized for conveying an even harder line on Taiwan. This issue was not the subject of obvious treatment or an intensive propaganda campaign likely to catch foreign attention. On the contrary, except for the "2/28" anniversary celebrations, Taiwan did not loom large in media messages.

Second, as a bargaining position, the regime presumably would want to hedge its position internally to leave some room for compromise so far as acceptability for domestic audiences was concerned. This could explain why more explicit language on the possible use of force distinguished private talks with American visitors from public media references. However, the maximum flexibility, including the possible failure to take any action in the absence of negotiatory agreement, could best be preserved by handling the Taiwan issue precisely as in the past. Instead, its importance was upgraded for domestic audiences. Moreover, to anticipate our discussion of developments after the January-April period, Peking finally published its three conditions for full diplomatic relations with Washington, thereby further lessening its domestic flexibility.

6. The hypothesis that changes in imagery on the U.S.-U.S.S.R. power relationship reflect a change in policy assessment is plausible and consistent with the available evidence. While the media data does not constitute proof, as a tentative explanation this deserves further examination.

Chinese communist confidence in the ability and will of the United States to confront the Soviet Union appeared to erode in 1975-76. [17] Mao's death removed a major constraint on foreign policy debate. To the extent that he and Chou had dictated the policy of Sino-American détente, their removal from the scene permitted its reexamination. A new consensus could emerge that would call into question the original assumptions which had underlain the Mao-Chou policy.

The coincidence of change on the Taiwan issue together with that on the U.S.-U.S.S.R. relationship strengthens this hypothesis. During the past several years, the decision to use the U.S. as a balance against the U.S.S.R. made muting of the Taiwan issue both necessary and justified. American sensitivity over the treaty commitment to the Chinese Nationalists precluded pressure on this point if the PRC-U.S. détente were to remain viable. Moreover, from 1968 to 1972, the Soviet threat was immediate; Taiwan remained a deferrable goal. Last but not least, in his first visit to China President Nixon personally committed himself to the "normalization of relations" during his second term.[18] Although this was not formalized in the Shanghai Communique of 28 February 1972, his private pledge would have carried considerable weight in Peking's policy councils. In contrast with western practice, Chinese relationships rely far more on interpersonal communications and confidence than on legalistic contracts.

However, this second aspect of Sino-American détente also came into doubt in 1974-76. Muting the issue failed to achieve the anticipated break in Taiwan's military and political ties with the United States. On the contrary, as highlighted in the Sino-American documents and chronology published in Hong Kong, these ties remained the same or were marginally strengthened. Therefore, if the tempering of Chinese statements on Taiwan was no longer necessitated by the advantages of détente linked to the strategic power balance, it was also not justified by the development of Taiwan-American relations.

Epilogue

Subsequent to completion of the formal research for this study which focused on January-April 1977, further developments in domestic media treatment of the themes under examination strengthened the original inferences. These developments warrant attention before placing our findings in a larger frame of reference.

The negative imagery concerning the United States took on a harsher tone in connection with articles highlighting the publication of

Mao Tse-tung's fifth volume of selected work. Placing special emphasis on the "Aid Korea, Resist America" movement, JMJP recalled how "U.S. aggressors brought the flames of war to China's borders after frenziedly overrunning vast areas in North Korea and continuously used their aircraft to bomb and strafe China's cities and towns, killing and wounding the peace-loving Chinese people and seriously threatening China's safety."[19]

After depicting the Chinese People's Volunteers' entry into the war, the article revived the accusation of germ warfare which dominated Chinese media in the early 1950s but had not been reiterated in recent years:

> Germ warfare is also known as "biological warfare."
> It is a barbarous means of war adopted by imperialists
> in wars of aggression to harm men, farm animals, and
> crops with all types of germs and viruses through means
> of insects, gases, vapors, and other means. . . . The
> U.S. armed forces of aggression in Korea spread small-
> pox germs in certain insects carrying germs of plague,
> cholera, typhoid, and other contagious diseases over
> Korea and northeast China. The Korean-Chinese armed
> forces and people carried out a quarantine and public
> health movement to smash this germ warfare launched
> by the enemy.

Although this article appeared as "reference material for studying volume five," no mention of germ warfare occurs in the entire compendium. Three days later JMJP carried another item based on Mao's analysis of nuclear weapons, noting that "immediately after liberation, the Chinese people, in the face of the U.S. imperialists' nuclear black-mail threat to drop atomic bombs on China, marched across the Yalu River." However, nowhere in Mao's cited analysis does he specifically link "nuclear blackmail" with Chinese entry into the Korean War.

The theme of growing Soviet power compared with waning American military might won continued attention in articles devoted to the Committee on the Present Danger, NATO intelligence reports, and congressional testimony. A detailed compilation of comparative capabilities and defense investment in JMJP concluded:

> The Soviet-U.S. balance of forces has changed in favor
> of the Soviet Union over the past decade as an effect of

the law governing the uneven economic and political
development of capitalism. . . . On the whole the
present Soviet production capacity and technological
strength are still behind that of the United States but
its rate of economic accumulation and the speed of
growth are higher than the latter. The speed of
Soviet military buildup is faster and its momentum
bigger than the United States. . . . It has not only
overwhelmed the U.S. in conventional arms, but is
equal to the latter in nuclear weapons and shows
superiority in some aspects. . . . Since the beginning of the 1970's, the average annual growth rate
of its military spending has been almost three times
that of the United States.[20]

The ambivalence with which the United States is viewed as a quasi-
ally, given this disparaging assessment of its strength relative to that
of the Soviet Union, was nowhere more bluntly or authoritatively stated
than by Chairman Hua Kuo-feng in his report of 12 August to the
Eleventh Congress of the Chinese Communist Party (CCP). Citing
Lenin on defeating "the most powerful enemy" by "skillfully making use
without fail of every, even the smallest, 'rift' among the enemies,"
Hua stressed "taking advantage of every, even the smallest, opportunity
of gaining a mass ally, even though this ally be temporary, vacillating,
unstable, unreliable, and conditional."[21] Although the words were
Lenin's, their applicability to the United States could not be missed.

Hua also dealt with the Taiwan issue more bluntly than had any
previous public pronouncement except for the less prominent NCNA
account of Li Hsien-nien's conversation with Admiral Zumwalt of
4 July 1977:

If the relations between the two countries are to be
normalized, the United States must sever its so-called
diplomatic relations with the Chiang clique, withdraw
all its armed forces and military installations from
Taiwan and the Taiwan Straits area and abrogate its
so-called "mutual defense treaty" with the Chiang
clique. Taiwan Province is China's sacred territory.
We are determined to liberate Taiwan. When and how
is entirely China's internal affair which brooks no
foreign interference whatsoever.

In sum, nothing that appeared in the domestic media subsequent to April 1977 contradicted the concatenation of themes highlighted in our research. On the contrary, significant reinforcement was given to the unfavorable recollection of the past Sino-American power balance, and the adamant statement of Taiwan policy.

It is important to distinguish three types of statements in the media: (1) those addressed to foreign audiences; (2) those addressed to domestic audiences; and (3) those addressed to domestic audiences which are presumed to be monitored abroad as well. For instance, interviews by high officials such as Teng Hsiao-p'ing and Li Hsien-nien to American visitors are usually not made available to the Chinese people. Analytical articles in JMJP may be relayed abroad by radio, by NCNA, or by Peking Review. However, most of them remain confined to domestic circulation under circumstances which would not attract foreign attention, FBIS monitoring to the contrary notwithstanding. Finally, major policy statements by Chairman Hua or the foreign ministry clearly serve several functions, including the transmittal of positions to both domestic and foreign groups.

The first category and to a certain extent the third are susceptible to varying interpretation of motive, most notably "signalling" for the purpose of informing, deterring, bargaining, or otherwise influencing the behavior of other governments. But the second category clearly must be viewed in the more limited context of influencing domestic perceptions and behavior. To the maximum extent possible, this criterion has conditioned the selection of material in this study.

At a minimum, this material could not have encouraged expectations of a rapid or dramatic improvement in Sino-American relations, particularly so far as the issue of Taiwan is concerned. At a maximum, it may have been designed to discourage reliance on détente with the United States as a continuing solution to China's confrontation with the Soviet Union and to forewarn of the possibility that an impasse over Taiwan might persist well into the future.

In this regard the timing of these materials is significant, coming as they do after the inauguration of President Carter and the installation of Premier Hua Kuo-feng but before the anticipated initial visit of Secretary Vance in August 1977. It is worth noting that the one brief passage in Mao's fifth volume which explicitly addressed the question of recognition by Washington of the PRC was singled out for internal attention during the spring and summer of 1977.[22] Speaking in

January 1957, Mao declared:

> I still think it preferable to put off the establishment of
> diplomatic relations with the United States for some
> years. This will be more to our advantage. . . . We
> are in no hurry to establish diplomatic relations with
> the United States. We adopt this policy to deprive the
> United States of as much political capital as possible
> and put it in the wrong and in an isolated position. . . .
> Once I told an American in Yenan, the United States can
> go on withholding recognition of our government for a
> hundred years, but I doubt if it can withhold it in the
> 101st. One day the United States will have to establish
> diplomatic relations with us.[23]

As the only such statement in the 500-page publication, this need not
have been brought to the attention of Chinese officials. That it was so
featured suggests the reservations with which the post-Mao leadership
viewed prospective Sino-American relations as of mid-1977.

METHODOLOGICAL NOTE AND DATA APPENDICES

Coding and Counting Rules

Counting a Story

1. In the case of a news report filed by the NCNA, each release is counted as one story. The space of each story includes the text of the release, the headline, and the accompanying photograph, if any.

2. Where a news item that has one headline but carries "n" NCNA releases, each release is counted as one story. The space of each story then includes the text of the release, and one-nth of the space of the headline and the accompanying photograph.

3. In cases of news items that are not NCNA releases, i.e., special columns, commentaries, signed articles, editorials, or PRC official statements and announcements, each item with a column title or headline is counted as one story.

Counting a U.S. Story

1. A U.S. story is:

   a) a story with a specific reference to the United States, or its abbreviations or derivations (U.S.A., U.S., American) or a segment of the U.S. (e.g., New York) in its headline. Stories with headlines containing reference to "superpower," "imperialism," "capitalism," and "the West" are not counted as a U.S. story unless b) holds.

   b) in cases where there are no specific reference to U.S. in the headline, a story with one-third or more of its paragraphs having at least one specific reference to U.S. (Note: the quantity one-third is not just an arbitrary cut-off point. Using one-fourth as the criterion would include many stories on Soviet Union expansion in Africa and which specify only S.U. in the headline; using one-half as the criterion would exclude several stories on anti-U.S. imperialism in Latin America. Further, using one-third as the criterion has the highest agreement with the coding of U.S. stories in Current Background.)

30

2. Where a news item has a headline but more than one release, one of which is a U.S. story (e.g., British, French, U.S. workers strike), only the release on U.S. is counted as one U.S. story. The space of that U.S. story then includes the text of the release and the proportionate size of the headline and photograph space, e.g., if there are three releases, one of which is on U.S., then the U.S. story will include one-third of the total headline and photograph space.

Counting Unfavorable U.S. Stories

1. An unfavorable U.S. story is one that reports:

   a) U.S. domestic problems, including: (1) economic problems (e.g., U.S. trade deficit soars), (2) social problems (e.g., U.S. blacks commemorate assassination of Dr. Martin Luther King), (3) class struggle (e.g., U.S. workers continue struggle against capitalists) (Appendix B)

   b) U.S. acting as antagonist to: (1) China, (2) Asia, and (3) Latin America (Appendix E, section I)

Counting Favorable U.S. Stories

1. A favorable story is one that reports U.S. Government/group/individuals supporting/visiting/befriending PRC (Appendix C, section I)

2. Americans of Chinese descent supporting/visiting/befriending PRC is not counted as a favorable U.S. story.

Thematic Analysis (Appendices B, C, D, E)

1. Categories of thematic classification are derived from the headline, the first and last paragraphs.

2. Where a story has more than one theme, the one closest to the headline determines the theme of the story.

3. If the headline is unclear, the one closest to the first paragraph determines the theme of the story.

4. If both the headline and the first paragraph are indeterminate, the one closest to the last paragraph determines the theme of the story.

5. If the headline, first and last paragraphs are indeterminate, the theme that has modal space becomes the theme of the story.

APPENDIX A

FAVORABLE VS. UNFAVORABLE JMJP STORIES ON U.S.
1 JANUARY TO 30 APRIL 1976 AND 1977

	1976(y)	1977(x)	x–y
I. Unfavorable Stories on U.S.			
A. Internal: Economic crisis, social problems, class struggle (BI, II, III)*	29	21	−8
B. External: U.S. acting alone, as antagonist to rest of the world (EI)	29	11	−18
Subtotal, unfavorable references:	58	32	−26
II. Favorable Stories on U.S.			
A. U.S. Government/Group/ Individuals supporting/ visiting/befriending PRC (CI)	43	20	−23
B. U.S. supports/concedes to Third World demands (EII)	5	6	+1
C. U.S. supports other nations to resist U.S.S.R. expansion (DII)	1	5	+4
Subtotal, favorable references:	49	31	−18

*Parenthetical references indicate specific sections of the
following appendices; e.g., BI refers to Appendix B,
section I.

APPENDIX B

JMJP COVERAGE OF U.S.--INTERNAL CONDITIONS
1 JANUARY TO 30 APRIL 1976 AND 1977

	1976					1977				
	Jan.	Feb.	Mar.	Apr.	+	Jan.	Feb.	Mar.	Apr.	= Total
I. Economic Crisis in the West and U.S.										
A. Headline reference to West, no reference to U.S., content reference to U.S. economic problem	1	3	–	2		1	1	2	–	
B. Headline reference to U.S., content reference to economic problem	–	2	3	–		1	–	1	1	
Subtotal:				11	+				7	= 18
II. Social Problems, Class Struggle in U.S.										
A. IB*, plus reference to working class suffering under capitalist exploitation	–	2	–	–		2	2	–	–	
B. IA, plus headline reference to U.S. proletariat/teachers/students resist/strike against capitalist exploitation, demand for better working conditions, settlement for grievances	2	2	5	3		1	1	2	2	
C. IIB, content reference	–	1	–	–		–	–	–	–	
D. Headline/content reference to U.S. racial problems: dominant class persecuting minor...	–	–	–	–		1	1	–	–	
E. Headline reference to U.S., content reference to U.S. government affiliation with exploiting/capitalist class	–	–	–	–		1	–	–	–	

F. IIA, plus reference to Soviet Union guilty of same   –   –   –   1   –

G. IID, plus reference to Soviet Union guilty of same   –   1   –   –   –

H. Reference to U.S. progressive in past, but has turned reactionary   1   –   –   –   –

Subtotal: 17 +   14 = 31

III. Spill-over effect of U.S. internal development in international scene

A. IB, plus content reference to U.S. transferring effects of economic crisis to Third World   1   –   –   –   –

Subtotal: 1 +   0 = 1

---

*IB refers to section I, circumstance A of this appendix; IIB to section II, circumstance B, and so on.

APPENDIX C

JMJP COVERAGE OF U.S.--EXTERNAL U.S./PRC RELATIONS

	1976				+	1977				= Total
	Jan.	Feb.	Mar.	Apr.		Jan.	Feb.	Mar.	Apr.	
I. U.S. Government/Groups/Individuals Supporting PRC										
A. Headline reference to U.S. pro-PRC group supporting PRC domestic developments	3	-	1	-		4	1	1	1	
B. Headline reference to U.S. Government dominant class visiting/supporting/befriending PRC	12	17	1	9		2	-	1	10	
Subtotal:				43	+				20	= 63
II. Government Relations: Shanghai Communique/Normalization										
A. Headline reference to U.S., content reference to U.S. officials stating Shanghai Communique as guiding U.S.--Chinese relations	-	2	-	-		-	-	-	-	
B. Headline reference to U.S., content reference to pro-PRC group calling for normalization	-	-	-	-		-	-	1	-	
C. IIA, plus reference to U.S. officials stating normalization and/or hegemony a problem	-	-	-	-		1	1	-	-	
D. IIA, plus reference to U.S. officials stating opposition to normalization	-	-	1	-		-	-	-	-	
Subtotal:				3	+				3	= 6

APPENDIX D

JMJP COVERAGE OF U.S.--EXTERNAL U.S./S.U. BILATERAL RELATIONS

	1976				1977				
	Jan.	Feb.	Mar.	Apr. +	Jan.	Feb.	Mar.	Apr.	= Total
I. S.U. an antagonist/rival/competitor of U.S.									
A. Headline reference to both in contention/ hostility/diplomatic offensive/verbal attack/ conventional or strategic arms development or race	1	2	4	–	–	6	8	1	
B. Headline reference to S.U. challenging/ threatening U.S. vital interests/spheres of influence/world position/security	3	–	–	–	2	3	–	1	
C. Headline reference to S.U.'s offensive, clandestine behavior towards U.S.	–	1	–	–	2	2	–	–	
D. Headline/content reference to both half-hearted/uncommitted to détente and arms limitation	–	–	–	1	–	–	5	11	
Subtotal:				12 +				41	= 53
II. U.S./S.U. strengths compared, no reference to détente									
A. Headline reference to both in contention, content reference to U.S. losing ground in world position to S.U.	–	2	–	–	–	–	–	–	
B. Headline/content reference to S.U. military expenditure as greater than that of U.S.	2	–	2	–	–	–	–	–	

Appendix D--continued

	1976				1977				= Total
	Jan.	Feb.	Mar.	Apr. +	Jan.	Feb.	Mar.	Apr.	
C. Headline reference to S.U. having achieved, or aims to achieve strategic superiority over U.S.	2	–	–	–	3	2	3	–	
D. IIC, but conventional superiority	–	–	–	2	–	–	–	–	
E. Headline reference to U.S. developing defense capabilities to offset S.U. attempt to achieve strategic superiority over U.S.	2	2	1	–	1	–	–	–	
F. Headline reference to U.S. and allies holding naval maneuvers	–	–	4	–	–	1	–	–	
Subtotal:				19 +				10	= 29
III. S.U. taking advantage of détente/arms limitation talks to seek hegemony, U.S./Europe wary of, and adopts hard-line									
A. Headline reference to U.S. and S.U., content reference to false détente and true contention between the two	–	–	1	–	1	1	–	–	
B. IIIA, plus reference to S.U. taking advantage of détente for military buildup and expansion	1	–	–	–	1	2	1	–	
C. IIIB, plus reference to S.U. aim to achieve strategic superiority over U.S.	–	–	–	–	–	–	–	1	

D. IIIB, plus reference to more U.S./European people aware of IIIA, advocating non-appeasement	8	2	2	1	1	6	-	-
E. IIIB, plus reference to more U.S. people aware of IIIC, and advocating non-appeasement	-	1	-	-	3	4	1	1
F. IIIC, plus reference that such will lead to world war	-	-	-	-	1	-	-	-
G. Headline reference to U.S./West economic aid to S.U. as fueling S.U. expansion	-	-	1	-	-	-	3	3
Subtotal:	17	+					30	= 47

APPENDIX E

JMJP COVERAGE OF U.S.--EXTERNAL
U.S./S.U./OTHER NATIONS

	1976				+	1977				= Total
	Jan.	Feb.	Mar.	Apr.		Jan.	Feb.	Mar.	Apr.	
I. U.S. acting alone, as antagonist to Second/Third World, to individual nations/peoples, as offender/accomplice										
A. Headline reference to U.S. as offender to other nations, acting as imperialist	2	4	10	5		1	6	2	2	
B. IA, but no headline reference, only content reference	–	2	–	–		–	–	–	–	
C. No headline reference to U.S., only content reference to U.S. as accomplice of/supporting reactionary regime in Third World	2	–	–	–		1	–	1	–	
D. IC, plus headline reference to U.S. as accomplice	1	–	–	–		–	–	–	–	
E. Headline reference to Third World making progress in struggle against superpowers, content reference to U.S. as antagonist of Third World	–	–	1	–		–	–	2	–	
Subtotal:				27	+				15	= 42
II. U.S. supports/concedes to Third World demands										
A. Headline reference to U.S. pro-Third World group supporting Third World demands	–	–	2	–		–	–	1	1	

							+				=	
B. Headline reference to U.S. government aiding/conceding to/conciliates with/engages in diplomacy with Third World nations	–	–	–	–	–		+	5	–	–		=	
Subtotal:					6		+	5				=	11
III. Both U.S./S.U. antagonistic to Third World nations/groups, with conflicting interests between superpowers													
A. Headline reference to U.S. and S.U., content reference to both being antagonistic to Third World, degree undifferentiated	1	3	1	–	2		+	–	–	–			
B. IIIA, headline reference to S.U.	–	1	–	–	–		+	–	–	–			
C. No headline reference to U.S., content reference to U.S. as chief antagonist to nation/people of Third World, non-Asia, with S.U. guilty of same	–	–	–	–	3		+	–	–	–			
D. IIIC, headline reference to U.S.	–	1	–	–	–		+	–	–	–			
E. Headline reference to superpower contention endangering stability of region, threatening interest and security of lesser powers in Second and Third World	1	1	1	–	–		+	3	5	4			
Subtotal:	6				16		+	3	5	4	17	=	33
IV. Both superpowers are, but S.U. is especially antagonistic to Third World, acting with conflicting interests													

Appendix E—continued

	1976 Jan.	Feb.	Mar.	Apr.	+ 1977 Jan.	Feb.	Mar.	Apr.	= Total
A. Headline reference to antagonism between superpowers and Third World, content reference to S.U./U.S. contention, in world in general	1	1	-	-	1	-	-	-	
B. IVA, contention in Asia	1	-	-	-	3	-	-	-	
C. IVA, contention outside Asia	13	-	-	-	4	-	2	-	
D. Headline reference to two superpower contention non-Asia (N. Europe)	-	-	-	-	-	1	-	-	
E. Headline reference to superpower contention being source of world/regional instability, and origin of new world war	3	3	6	-	6	1	-	-	
F. Headline reference to superpowers feigning détente and SALT to limit smaller powers' nuclear program to achieve nuclear monopoly, at the same time expanding their own nuclear arsenal	-	-	-	-	1	-	-	-	
G. Headline reference to superpowers' position on 200 mile limit as against the economic interest of Third World nations	-	-	-	-	-	-	1	-	
Subtotal:				28	+			20	= 48

V. Both superpowers are antagonistic to Third World, but S.U. is singled out as the great/most dangerous enemy and source of new world war

A. Reference to S.U. a scoundrel/great enemy/most dangerous enemy/war monger and neo-colonialist/no. 1 arms salesman	–	2	1	–	3	–	–	–	–
B. Reference to S.U. as source of new world war/aiming to achieve superiority over U.S./conquer Europe	–	–	1	1	1	–	1	1	–
C. Reference to S.U. as sole actor in an event that disrupts international/regional order, or preserves status quo	–	–	–	–	–	–	–	3	–
D. VC, plus reference that U.S. did not participate in event and protested S.U. action	1	–	–	–	–	–	–	–	–
Subtotal:			6	+				8	= 14
VI. U.S. supports other nations to resist S.U. expansion									
A. Headline reference to U.S. supporting other nations, content reference to support aimed at defending nation against S.U. expansion	–	–	–	–	–	–	–	–	1
B. VIA, no headline reference to U.S.	–	–	–	–	–	–	–	–	1
C. VIB, plus reference to European nations advocating building up its own forces and making greater contribution to their own defense to guard against S.U. threat	–	–	1	–	–	–	–	1	1
D. VIC, plus reference to U.S. support to European defense as being insufficient	–	–	–	–	–	–	–	1	–
Subtotal:			1	+				5	= 6

Appendix E—continued

VII. Both superpowers, acting in converging interests, are antagonistic to other nations

| | 1976 | | | | + | 1977 | | | | = Total |
	Jan.	Feb.	Mar.	Apr.		Jan.	Feb.	Mar.	Apr.	
A. Content reference to current convergence of interests	2	1	–	1	+	–	1	–	–	
B. Content reference to past converging interests and present contention	1	–	–	–		–	–	–	–	
Subtotal:	5				+	1				= 6

VIII. Total number of JMJP stories involved

	1976	1977
January	71	55
February	58	46
March	50	57
April	32	43
	211	201

APPENDIX F

PROSPECTS AND DETERMINATION OF LIBERATION OF TAIWAN (TERMINOLOGY)
1 JANUARY TO 30 APRIL 1976 AND 1977

(Numbers indicate frequency of occurrence in this period except two days before and after 2/28)
([ ] numbers indicate frequency of occurrence in this period two days before and after 2/28)

	JMJP 1976	JMJP 1977	FBIS 1976	FBIS 1977	76-77 Total*	76-77 Grand Total
I. No reference to liberation prospects or determination					+8	+9
A. Evil/weakness of Taiwan					+2	+3
1. Colony of U.S. economy imperialism			3			
2. Reactionary literature and art		1	1			
3. Plight of women	1	1		1		
4. Reactionary educational system	[1]			1		
5. Poor nuclear strength		1	1			
6. Drought		1	1			
7. Expensive medical care				1		
B. Situation Worsening					+6	+6
1. General (political, social, economic)	1		3			
2. Economy	1		1			
C. PRC shows consideration/leniency/ warm reception to Taiwan compatriots					0	0
1. Fisherman in distress		1	1	1		

*This column excludes those occurrences appearing two days before and after 2/28.

Appendix F-- continued

	JMJP 1976	JMJP 1977	FBIS 1976	FBIS 1977	76-77 Total	76-77 Grand Total
2. Released KMT personnel			3	1		
3. Suspend shelling to offshore islands	1	2	2	2	0	0
D. Other						
1. Taiwan students in U.S. learnt about PRC		1	1			
II. Statement of Wish/Belief in Liberation of Taiwan					0	0
A. Liberation of Taiwan the common wish of Chinese people			1			
B. Taiwan people long for liberation		1	1	1		
III. Liberation of Taiwan due to non-PRC forces					+6	+6
A. Liberation of Taiwan is inevitable	[1]		1			
B. Taiwan people struggling for liberation	1		2	[1]		
C. Call on Taiwan military and political personnel to contribute to liberation			2			
IV. Expression of Determination and Commitment					-3	-9
A. Pledge of contribution to liberation made by Taiwan compatriots	[2]	[2]	1			
B. Pledge of contribution to liberation made by Chinese in mainland	1	3		1 [1]		
C. Pledge of contribution to liberation made by released former KMT personnel who returned to mainland				1		

	C1	C2	C3	C4	C5	C6
D. Statement of determination to liberate Taiwan	1	[6]	[1]	1	0	+1
V. Statement of Futility of/Warning against outside interference						
A. Outside interference schemes futile (always appear with IV, D)	[3]	[1]	[3]	[2]		
B. Liberation of Taiwan is the internal affair of the Chinese that brooks no foreign interference				[2]		
VI. Expression of Urgency					-7	-8
A. Taiwan compatriots long for/resolved to contribute to the early liberation of Taiwan		1	[1]	1		
B. Taiwan compatriots in Japan/U.S./China resolved to contribute to the early liberation of Taiwan		5		[2]		
VII. Hint that use of force in liberation may not be excluded					-1	-3
A. "If things develop to such a stage that no problem can be solved without armed conflict"				1		
B. "The absurd proposition that the liberation of Taiwan should not be accomplished by use of force should be condemned"		[1]				
C. Mao quote, "IF THE BROOM IS NOT THERE, THE DUST AS A RULE WILL NOT DISAPPEAR BY ITSELF."		[1]				

APPENDIX G

FBIS ON TAIWAN
1 JANUARY TO 30 APRIL 1976 AND 1977

	1976	1977
I. Internal Broadcasts		
A. Peking Domestic NCNA in Chinese	5	4
B. Foochow, Fukien Province in Mandarin	1	1
C. Hangchow, Chekiang Province in Mandarin	–	1
Subtotal:	6 (20.6%)	6 (35.3%)
II. External Broadcasts		
A. Fukien Front PLA in Mandarin to Taiwan	5	1
B. Peking in Mandarin to Taiwan	9	–
C. Peking NCNA in English	8	10
D. Hong Kong Wen Hui Pao	1	–
Subtotal:	23 (79.4%)	11 (64.7%)
Total:	29	17

NOTES

Introduction

1. These studies were completed under Department of State Contract,
    No. 1722-620042. However, they do not represent the views of the
    United States government. Mr. James Tong served as research
    assistant for the analysis of PRC media images. Mr. W. K. Chan
    was a research assistant for the analysis of whole plant imports.

2. An excellent example of this approach is Thomas M. Gottlieb,
    Chinese Foreign Policy Factionalism and the Origins of the
    Strategic Triangle (Santa Monica: The Rand Corporation, R-1902-
    NA, November 1977).

3. For further commentary on this matter, see Allen S. Whiting,
    "Chinese Foreign Policy: A Workshop," Social Science Research
    Council, Items (March/June 1977): 1-3.

4. For a critical review of the literature, see Harry Harding,
    "Domestic Linkages to Foreign Policy" (Manuscript presented to
    the Chinese Foreign Policy Workshop, Ann Arbor, MI, August 1976).
    Among the more rigorous empirical studies, Peter Van Ness,
    Revolution and Chinese Foreign Policy (Berkeley: University of
    California Press, 1970) and Roy F. Grow, The Politics of Industrial
    Development in China and the Soviet Union: Organizational Strategy
    as a Linkage Between National and World Politics (Ann Arbor:
    University Microfilms, 1973) deserve special mention.

5. The author resided in Hong Kong in 1954-55 and 1966-68.

6. See, for example, Michael Y. M. Kau, ed., The Lin Piao Affair
    (White Plains, N. Y.: International Arts and Sciences Press, Inc.,
    1975); also various issues of Issues and Studies (Taipei: Institute
    of International Affairs).

7. The most complete study of the available <u>chung-fa</u> is Kenneth Lieberthal, <u>Central Documents and Politburo Politics in China</u>, Michigan Papers in Chinese Studies, no. 33 (Ann Arbor, 1978).

8. The closest analysis of this material is in Robert Sutter, <u>China-Watch: Sino-American Reconciliation</u> (Baltimore: Johns Hopkins University Press, 1978). See also J. D. Armstrong, <u>Revolutionary Diplomacy: Chinese Foreign Policy and the United Front Doctrine</u> (Berkeley: University of California Press, 1977), pp. 98-104.

9. The most extensive collection of PRC classified materials pertaining to foreign policy is in J. Chester Cheng, <u>The Politics of the Chinese Red Army</u> (Stanford: Hoover Institution, 1966).

10. The author spent 1974-75 in Taiwan examining purported PRC materials held by appropriate agencies with the kind permission of the Republic of China authorities. Particular attention was given to documents allegedly issued between July 1971 and May 1975. In a few cases original copies were made available but most were already transcribed and reprinted in standard form rather than in simplified characters. The author wishes to express his appreciation to the Social Science Research Council for a fellowship which made this research possible.

11. See, for instance, the alleged 42,000-word test of a 30 July 1977 foreign policy address attributed to PRC Foreign Minister Huang Hua and distributed by the Chinese Information Service, Republic of China, 26 December 1977. Hua's reassurance that "even when China-U.S. relations are normalized, the U.S.-Taiwan mutual defense treaty is invalidated, and U.S. forces are withdrawn from Taiwan, we will not, within the next decade, use force to liberate Taiwan," would, if believed, encourage Washington to break diplomatic and military ties with Taipei. However, senior officials in the Carter administration privately informed the author they were confident the document was not authentic.

12. A senior intelligence analyst in the U.S. government expressed disbelief in the authenticity of an alleged speech by Keng Piao, "Keng Piao's Talks on 'A Turning Point in The China-U.S. Diplomatic Relations' (Excerpts)" <u>Issues and Studies</u> (January 1977). One item examined by the author in Taiwan allegedly in the original text showed inconsistencies in calligraphy. Another reversed the sequential order of a standard formulation. A third contained a fatal anachronism.

13. For the best defense and application of nonquantitative content analysis, see Donald S. Zagoria, The Sino-Soviet Conflict, 1956-1961 (Princeton: Princeton University Press, 1962). The use of quantitative content analysis for domestic politics is central in Paul J. Hiniker, Revolutionary Ideology and Chinese Reality: Dissonance Under Mao (Beverly Hills: Sage Publications, 1977). For nonquantitative analysis of Chinese foreign policy, see Gottlieb, Chinese Foreign Policy Factionalism; also Kenneth Lieberthal, Sino-Soviet Relations in 1970's (Santa Monica: The Rand Corporation, 1978). A good example of its application to English versions of Chinese texts is offered in Armstrong, Revolutionary Diplomacy.

14. See testimony of A. Doak Barnett, 2 and 24 February 1976 in United States-China Relations: The Process of Normalization of Relations, Hearings Before The Special Subcommittee on Investigations of the Committee on International Relations, House of Representatives, 94th Congress; also Thomas Robinson, "Political and Strategic Aspects of Chinese Foreign Policy," in China and Japan: A New Balance of Power: Critical Choices For Americans, ed. Donald Hellman (Lexington: D. C. Heath, 1976); Allen S. Whiting, "Now, Closer U.S. Relations With China--Perhaps," The New York Times, 17 October 1976.

15. For specific allegations of Yao Wen-yuan's manipulation of the media to suppress the news of mourning for Chou En-lai, see Peking NCNA in English, 7 January 1977 and in Mandarin, 6 January 1977, in FBIS, 11 January 1977; original and fuller charges in JMJP, 6 January, 9 January, 14 January, and 26 January 1977; also 25 March 1977.

16. See Allen S. Whiting, China Crosses The Yalu (Stanford: Stanford University Press, 1968), chapter 6 and The Chinese Calculus of Deterrence (Ann Arbor: University of Michigan Press, 1975) (hereafter Chinese Calculus), chapter 7.

17. Chinese Calculus, chapter 3.

18. See Mao Tse-tung, Mao Tse-tung ssu-hsiang wan-sui! [Long Live the Thought of Mao Tse-tung] (August 1969; reprinted photographically by the Institute of International Relations, Taipei, June 1973), speech to cooperative heads, 30 November 1958, p. 255, "NATO is attacking nationalism and its own communism . . . but towards the socialist camp it is defensive even in the Hungarian incident. But our propaganda is another matter and

we must still say they are attacking. We must not deceive ourselves by this propaganda." Other examples can be found in speeches between 1956 and 1958. This collection was clandestinely acquired from unidentified mainland sources and originally distributed as an unauthorized Red Guard compilation. While individual words may not be accurately recorded, the gist of his remarks can be relied upon as evidenced by subsequent PRC publication of numerous documents contained therein, especially in Mao Tse-tung, Selected Works (Peking: Foreign Languages Press, 1977), vol. V.

19. An American visitor to China in October 1976 asked his guide whether there were any male announcers because it seemed that all the local broadcasts relayed through loudspeakers were made by women. The guide replied, "Oh yes, we use men for really important announcements." Recounted to the author.

20. Mr. James Tong conceived of this research technique.

21. Mr. James Tong served as research assistant for this study, undertaken in support of a Japanese-American Korean project directed by Dr. Franklin Weinstein, Stanford University.

22. JMJP, 7 August 1977.

23. In some instances, as long as two years have elapsed between the initial Chinese contact with a foreign supplier and the final signing of a contract.

Part I

1. See, for instance, "Change in PRC Leadership, Current Propaganda Suggests Continued Moderate Peking Policy Toward U.S.," FBIS Special Memorandum, 27 December 1976.

2. The Hong Kong newspaper, Ming Pao, 30 October 1976 (FBIS, 6 November 1976), carried an alleged denunciation of the Gang made by Hua Kuo-feng, Yeh Chien-ying, and Wang Tung-hsing at a Politburo meeting which claimed, "The 'gang of four' had all along resisted and attempted to sabotage the revolutionary

diplomatic line set forth by Chairman Mao himself . . . [and] vilified and undermined the united front work conducted diplomatically in regards to the Western countries." This report cannot be verified but other Ming Pao versions of mainland materials subsequently proved essentially correct. It must be noted, however, that the author has no knowledge of any anti-Gang materials which explicitly cite obstruction of Sino-American détente.

3. Hong Kong Agence France Presse in English citing Georges Biannic, Peking, 29 October 1976, in FBIS, 1 November 1976.

4. Professor Michael Lampton, Ohio State University, kindly provided this information.

5. Kuang-sheng Liao and Allen S. Whiting, "Chinese Press Perceptions of Threat: The U.S. and India, 1962," The China Quarterly, no. 53 (January/March 1973): 80–89.

6. These views were given to the U.S. World Affairs Delegation, headed by Mr. Cyrus Vance, in October 1975 by Vice-Premier Teng Hsiao-p'ing, Acting Foreign Minister Han Nien-lung, and others; the author accompanied this group.

7. "Learn from Premier Chou's Brilliant Example, Strive to Carry Out Chairman Mao's Revolutionary Line in Foreign Affairs," Jen-min Jih-pao, 11 January 1977; full translation in Survey of People's Republic of China Press (SPRCP), no. 6265 (24 January 1977); see also Peking Review, no. 5 (28 January 1977).

8. SPRCP, no. 6265 (24 January 1977): 2.

9. Peking Review, no. 5 (28 January 1977): 7–8.

10. Ibid., p. 11.

11. The author's attention was specifically drawn to this article in these terms by an official in the PRC Liaison Office in Washington D.C.

12. FBIS Trends, 2 March 1977.

13. FBIS Trends, 19 January 1977.

14. Chung-mei kuan-hsi wen-chien hui-pien [Documentary Collection on Sino-American Relations] (Hong Kong: Ch'i Shih Nien Tai Yueh K'an, March 1977).

15. Jen-min Jih-pao, 17 January 1977, article by Taiwan Province Sports Work Liaison Office, National Sports Federation of China, "Beloved Premier Chou, Taiwan Compatriots Remember You." Emphasis in the original.

16. Forthcoming research by Professor Kenneth Lieberthal under auspices of the Rand Corporation argues this point with respect to Sino-Soviet relations.

17. This dominated presentations made in Peking during October and December 1975 during the aforementioned visit by the Vance delegation, the coincidental visit of Secretary of State Kissinger, and the subsequent visit of President Ford.

18. The New York Times, 11 April 1977, attributed to administration sources.

19. Jen-min Jih-pao, 10 May 1977, in FBIS, 25 May 1977.

20. Jen-min Jih-pao, 20 August 1977, in FBIS, 22 August 1977.

21. Peking Review, no. 35 (26 August 1977).

22. The author learned of this in Hong Kong and was confirmed in his knowledge by an official in the PRC Liaison Office in Washington, D.C.

23. Selected Works of Mao Tse-tung, vol. V (Peking: Foreign Language Press, 1977), p. 363.

Domestic Politics and Foreign Trade
in the PRC, 1971-1976

Project Design

This study examines the relevance of domestic politics in the PRC
for determining the importation of whole plants during the period 1971-
76.* This particular aspect of Chinese foreign trade became significant
in dollar volume and material content in 1973-74 but dropped sharply in
1975 and virtually stopped in 1976. Economic analysis attributed the
sudden decline to the impact of worldwide inflation on China's imports
and worldwide recession on its exports, coupled with the anticipated
cumulative indebtedness of contracts signed in 1972-74. The PRC
balance of payments deficit rose from approximately $83 million in 1973
to more than $900 million in 1974. Political analysis stressed instead
the emergence of public criticism against reliance on foreign technology
in 1974 which increased in 1975, and reached a peak in the "anti-Teng"
movement of 1976.

Both analyses have considerable prima facie merit. Economic
constraints are severe so long as China refuses to accept long-term
loans or credit. Its large agricultural economy is subject to the visis-
situdes of weather, which affect industrial and food crops that in turn
affect production and consumption. The impact on foreign trade is felt
in both the availability of exports and the need for grain imports. These
interrelationships call for caution in signing fixed payment contracts
for costly imports over a future of several years because without re-
course to long-term loans or credit, the potential disruption of agriculture could limit industrial exports and increase imports of foodstuffs.
Moreover, as already noted, the sudden inflationary surge of import
prices and recessionary shrinkage of export markets in 1974-75

*I am deeply indebted to Mr. W. K. Chan for his invaluable research
assistance and to Professor Robert Dernberger for his critical com-
ments and generous use of unpublished manuscripts.

adversely affected China's trade balance even before payments on already signed contracts were scheduled to begin.

Historical precedent adds a further cause for concern. The Chinese experience with the importation of foreign plants and technology has been mixed from both an economic and political point of view. Aside from the century of foreign concessions, consortia, and protected investment prior to 1949, the following decade of Soviet dependence left a bitter heritage of financial indebtedness, economic subservience, and political humiliation. The credits advanced by Stalin and Khrushchev came due for repayment just when the Chinese economy was reeling from the backlash of Mao's blunders in the Great Leap Forward and three years of successive natural disasters. During the depths of China's recession in 1961-62 much of the country suffered from malnutrition but exports of pork and grain to the Soviet Union continued until the debt was fully retired in 1964. Moreover, the Soviet equipment was of mixed quality, including modern developments in steel production and antiquated machine-tool items. Last but not least, in July 1960 Khrushchev suddenly removed all the Soviet technicians and blueprints because of his political dispute with Mao, leaving many plants incomplete and depriving others of necessary advisors for installation and maintenance.

By focusing on whole plants exclusively, rather than the importation of all machinery and equipment normally included in technology transfer, we highlight the political aspects of economic relationships. Whereas individual items purchased abroad may be easily installed and operated in Chinese factories, the acquisition of a petrochemical complex or an advanced steel mill raises social and economic questions beyond the immediate problems of cost and productivity. For example, the technological imperatives of modern industrial installations mitigate against management by the masses. Narrow tolerances for variation in the quality of materials utilized, speed of operation, environmental pollution and temperature, and routine maintenance may preclude decisions on such matters by anyone without the requisite training. Even the basic decision on when and where to install the plant may require a thorough understanding of its optimum operating environment.

The initial transfer of Soviet equipment to the PRC in the late 1940s evoked conflicting models of worker-management relations and industrial development as between those envisioned by Mao and what actually evolved under Kao Kang in northeast China.[1] The prerogatives of a specialized managerial elite clashed with concepts of an egalitarian mass line. Moreover, the location of heavy industry, while rational in economic terms, carried political implications that were contrary to aspirations for growth and modernization elsewhere.

The Great Leap Forward of 1958-60 reasserted the priority of politics over economics and revolution in relationships over efficiency in production. This ethos argued against allocating authority to experts and calculating investment in terms of cost-benefit analysis. The vigor with which ideological values were again reasserted in the Cultural Revolution, rejecting technologically oriented methods, suggests the depths of resistance--at least in Mao and his closest associates--to compromising social goals in order to maximize economic gains.

An additional problem posed by the importation of whole plants is the likely need for foreign technicians to supervise installation and maintenance during the initial period of operation or, alternatively, the training of Chinese technicians in foreign countries. In a society of poverty and scarcity, the presence of individuals with higher living standards, if only manifest in clothes and personal possessions, can arouse resentment. In contemporary China where the emphasis on personal abstemiousness serves as a rationale for low wages and few consumer goods, foreign residents offer a potentially subversive image of lifestyle.[2] An even greater risk attends the assignment of Chinese abroad for prolonged periods of inservice training.

Furthermore, the universal desire for self-esteem is ultimately predicated on self-reliance, a concept which has been central in the PRC since 1949 when Mao Tse-tung proclaimed, "New China has stood up!" Its roots extend back through the centuries of China's self-proclaimed centrality as the Middle Kingdom. The end of empire introduced the "century of shame and humiliation," so called by Nationalists and Communists alike because of China's subservience to and dependence on foreign powers. Whether in military, economic, political, or ideological matters, the foreign advisor played a preeminent role. In the suppression of the Taiping rebellion, the management of customs, the founding of the Chinese Communist Party, its fusion with the Kuomintang and the undertaking of the Northern Expedition, down to the laying of the industrial base for "New China" and the start of its atomic weapons program, Chinese had to swallow their pride and do what the foreigner said. Residual resentment against this past carries serious implications for the present.

Finally, the cost of whole plants is significantly greater than for machinery and equipment in smaller packages. This factor can enlarge the dependency relationship with the foreign entrepreneur if the transaction requires financial underwriting or support by his government. For instance, Export-Import Bank sanction in Washington or Tokyo raises the prospect of political considerations which might constrain Peking's foreign policy options. Government controls over licensing and restrictions over exports where matters of security arise add additional constraints. Even after approval and financing are granted, a continuing requirement for spare parts, replacements, or major repair could place leverage in the hands of foreign governments. From 1950 to 1971/72, the United States trade embargo served as a constant reminder of how an opponent could seek to manipulate China's economic vulnerability for political ends.

As a point of principle, the PRC leadership steadfastly refused to seek foreign loans outside the socialist bloc or to grant foreign concessions and joint-stock companies other than those extracted by Stalin in his initial bargaining with Mao in 1950. To the extent possible, the goal of balanced trade conditioned import policy.[3] Conservative economics and sensitive politics determined overall policy.

Despite these economic and political considerations, however, the PRC undertook a major program of importing whole plants and advanced technology in 1972-75. The reasons were compelling. Soviet bloc equipment sufficed for the initial industrial base laid down after postwar reconstruction but was inadequate for the next stage of economic growth. It was also becoming obsolete. Nearly twenty years of use, often under conditions of mismanagement and poor maintenance, further lessened its utility. In addition, China's military defense remains vulnerable so long as the domestic production of modern aircraft, missiles, and tanks is hampered by a weak industrial base.

Yet the program faced definite obstacles. Because the economy remained basically agricultural, supplemented by light industry, exports were unlikely to fund a sufficient volume of imports to meet the need for new plants and equipment. This in turn forced reliance on the export of natural resources, such as coal and oil, together with some form of deferred payment in lieu of long-term loans or credits which were excluded by policy. But the diversion of natural resources from domestic to foreign consumption touched a sensitive nationalistic nerve and acceptance of deferred payments ran the risk of a recurring trade imbalance as unforeseeable circumstances lowered export earnings.

These factors make foreign trade a potentially contentious topic from a political as well as an economic point of view. Indicators of such contention are likely to be indirect, however, if policy already approved at the center is opposed by a losing or minority faction. Debate on contemporary issues may be masked by historical analogy with past Chinese experience, recent or remote. Clues to controversy often lie in key phrases and subtle nuances. For instance, articles on foreign trade carried critical references to "worshipping foreign things," "being servile to foreign things," "having a slavish comprador mentality" and "following behind at a snail's pace." These could have different connotations, depending on the context. Similarly, the juxtaposition of "using foreign things" versus "practicing self-reliance" may be accompanied by greater emphasis on either principle, thereby negating the other.

The appearance of such code words does not automatically signal controversy. They initially gained wide circulation as routine indictments of Liu Shao-ch'i in media campaigns that employed repetitive formulations without any special guidance beyond an initial directive. They also occurred in connection with the periodic drive for greater initiative on the part of local industry and individual workers to utilize local resources and ingenuity for technical innovation. Thus, beyond a simple quantitative content analysis, care must be given to the context within which these phrases occur.

This context includes the actual process of China's importation of whole plants extending from the initial contact with foreign sources through the signing of contracts, installation, and repayment. Although it is impossible to pinpoint the precise moment of decision to undertake a particular import program or to sign an individual contract, reasonable inferences can be drawn by reconstructing the pattern of negotiations. These inferences can then be placed against the larger framework of Peking's balance of trade and changing conditions in the international economy. Political factors, particularly factional controversy which involved foreign trade, are then weighed against these economic considerations.

This study examines the hypothesis that in the long-standing confrontation between two factions or coalitions headed respectively by Chou En-lai and Chiang Ch'ing, foreign trade became an important issue. Post hoc accusations against Chiang Ch'ing's Gang of Four would appear to confirm the hypothesis. However, these accusations fell far short of a full account, especially on the rhythm of decision and debate, an important datum in attempting to discriminate between economic and political considerations. Moreover, the voluminous charges against the Gang of Four included so much exaggeration, if

not fabrication, that they could not be accepted at face value without
some effort at independent corroboration.

The initial search for references to foreign trade scanned the
translated materials issued by the American Consulate General in Hong
Kong and FBIS for the period 1971-76. The more important items were
then examined in their original Chinese language source. In addition,
valuable information and guidance were provided by the staff and facilities of the Office of East Asian Affairs in the Bureau of Intelligence and
Research, Department of State.

PRC Whole Plant Imports

Peking's initial venture into the importation of whole plants,
following the termination of Soviet deliveries in 1960, occurred in the
years 1963-66. More than $200 million worth of contracts were
signed for over fifty whole plants, almost half of which were agreed
to in 1965.[4] Western Europe, Scandinavia, and Japan were to provide facilities for the production of petrochemicals, fertilizer, syn-
thetic fiber, steel, metallurgical and automotive goods. The terms
ranged from full cash to only 15 percent down payment with five years
for completion. Foreign technicians performed site inspection and
installation.

This program suddenly ended with the onset of the Cultural
Revolution, although it had not evoked any previous public indicators
of controversy. Subsequently, Liu Shao-ch'i, Mao's presumed successor prior to 1966 but then castigated as "China's Khrushchev," was
accused of "worshipping foreign things" and encouraging "a slavish
comprador mentality" designed to keep China "following at a snail's
pace." The virulent xenophobia which characterized Red Guard ram-
pages in Peking and Shanghai made conditions intolerable for foreign
negotiators and technicians. Some were imprisoned as secret agents;
others remained confined to their hotel rooms for many months. So
far as is known, few contracts were concluded in 1967 and several of
the larger earlier agreements simply faded away. Between 1968 and
1971 only ten contracts were signed for a total of $18 million.[5]

The Ninth Congress of the CCP in 1969 designated Lin Piao as
Mao's successor. The most turbulent period of the Cultural Revolution

had ended with suppression of the Red Guards and the creation of "three in one" revolutionary committees throughout the country. However, by 1971 the systematic narrowing of radical influence signalled a subtle shift of power from the newly risen mass representatives and radicals to the former cadres and moderates.[6] This shift climaxed with the fall of Lin Piao in September 1971 amidst official accusations of having conspired to assassinate Mao and being killed in an airplane accident on an attempted flight to the Soviet Union.

It is impossible to determine the actual time when decisions were made which led to the revived dependency on importation of foreign plants. Presumably central meetings in 1970-71 addressed the issue in connection with discussion of the Fourth Five Year Plan, although no specific information is available.[7] Also at this time the decision to exploit Soviet-American rivalry to offset a perceived Soviet threat to China culminated in the secret trip to Peking by Henry Kissinger in July 1971, arranging the visit by President Nixon in February 1972. This initial dialogue carried additional implications beyond the strategic interaction of Moscow-Washington-Peking. No longer would an American trade embargo bar nonstrategic goods, thereby permitting American licensed equipment heretofore excluded from third country sales to China to be accessible. It would also open the door to the most technologically advanced economy in the world. These considerations could not have escaped the attention of the leadership in Peking.

In addition to these logical inferences, the long lead times evidenced in Chinese behavior between initial discussions and the final signing of contracts suggests that the overall import policy was adopted no later than 1971. The first exploration of prospects for whole plant purchases occurred during the spring and fall of 1972.[8] This included inquiries for technical information in West Germany, soundings in France for two petrochemical plants in excess of $300 million, and discussion in Japan for a ball-bearing plant. Actual contracts in 1972 totalled $58 million. This activity indicated that a major program was underway for the acquisition of foreign technology. So significant a step must have been determined at the highest level during the previous year, if not earlier.

Both the cost and the content of the program expanded rapidly in the next two years, with $1.2 billion worth of contracts concluded in 1973 and another $850 million in 1974. However, in 1975 the program fell off sharply to $364 million, over half of which was for British jet fighter engine construction. In 1976, purchases amounted to less than

$200 million, almost all of which were signed during the first quarter of the year.[9]

The scope of the program as measured in terms of the sources of imports and their specific purpose further indicates that its initiation was decided upon during the final formulation of the Fourth Five Year Plan. Purchases occurred in Japan, France, the United Kingdom, the Netherlands, West Germany, Italy, Denmark, and the United States. Production facilities were acquired for ethylene and butadiene, polyethylene, polypropylene, polyester spinning, urea and ammonia, and bearings. Steel output benefitted from a hot strip rolling mill, a cold rolling mill, and a continuous casting mill, as well as equipment for silicon steel plate.[10] Hundreds of West German, French, Japanese, and American technicians were to supervise installation, train managers and operators, and advise on maintenance.

Payment was to be implemented over a five year period, usually commencing after actual production began. Because a year or two was frequently required for installation and test-runs, the full impact on China's balance of payments would not be felt before 1976-77. However, international economic conditions worsened sharply after the 1973 oil embargo. China faced rising import prices from inflation and a shrinking export market from recession. As a result, its trade balance suffered a deficit of $83 million in 1973 and soared to $900 million in 1974. While this did not yet involve major payments for whole plant imports, it provided an ominous forewarning of the difficulties that could lie ahead.

The trade deficit undoubtedly contributed to the slowdown in contracts concluded in 1975. An additional consideration presumably was the problem of absorbing these sizeable and complex purchases into the economy, particularly given China's limited technological elite and shortages in middle-level management.

In 1976 negotiations for whole plants ground to a halt. Contradictory explanations of policy were privately voiced to foreign traders following the death of Chou En-lai in January. Some officials referred to the trade imbalance and limits of absorption. Others infrequently mentioned "political difficulties" as impeding negotiations.[11] All exhibited unusual signs of uncertainty and anxiety, despite long experience and close familiarity with their foreign counterparts. Beginning in April, the campaign against Teng Hsiao-p'ing openly attacked the import program for the first time, although indirect criticism had occurred as early as 1974. The manifest political content of this attack raised the question of whether the reduction of foreign plant imports resulted from economic or political considerations, or both. The timing and wording of the attack also obscured precisely when the program had initially become controversial.

The foregoing synopsis provides the background for reexamining public media references to dependence on foreign technology and whole plant imports. Clues to controversy can be placed in context to evaluate their importance for decisions. Their relevance to ongoing political developments also warrants consideration. After surveying the evidence, better inferences can be drawn as to the relative role of economic and political factors in China's foreign trade during this particular period.

Chinese Media Survey: 1971-73

During the first three months of 1971 at least nine articles critical of foreign technology appeared in JMJP, Kuang-ming Jih-pao (KMJP), and NCNA. This "mini-campaign" is worthy of note. Although it did not purport to address an extant issue, certain words and phrases became the standard lexicon of subsequent political attack. As a keynote statement, JMJP of 6 January 1971 deserves quotation:

> Liu Shao-ch'i laid a "theoretical" foundation for the slavish comprador philosophy and the doctrine of crawling at a snail's pace. . . . He said preposterously: "We cannot get rid of foreign theories at one stroke because we do not have our own theories."
>
> . . . We must not blindly believe in foreign and old technology but must instead use the viewpoint of dividing one into two to give them a concrete analysis. As long as we can manifest the spirit of "using old things in a modern way and using foreign things in a way suited to local conditions," look at things of the past and things foreign with a scientific and critical eye . . . we shall be able to innovate those backward foreign old methods. [12]

It is possible that this article together with the other eight represented an oblique attack against the pending consideration of whole plant imports. Although there is no direct evidence of this subject being discussed at high levels, it might well have been raised at the Second Plenum of the Ninth CCP Central Committee, 23 August-6 September 1970. This meeting approved the State Council report on the National Planning Conference and the National Economic Plan for 1970. Another possible forum was the December 1970 meeting of the enlarged Politburo known as the "North China Conference."[13]

The code words "slavish comprador philosophy" and "crawling at a snail's pace" later became politically charged, specifically in connection with whole plant imports. The subsequent purchase of advanced equipment for metallurgy and mining calls attention to a March 1971 JMJP critique of such foreign items which alleged that "many of them are heavy and clumsy, involving high intensity labor and lacking safety and protective devices."[14] This charge probably referred to Soviet designed machinery but could have been more generally directed. Another article in the same issue attacked Liu for alleging that where mining equipment is concerned, "in the case of some new technologies, we can buy them from foreign countries after they get them ready; we need only to follow them."

If this line of attack were directed against a contemplated increase in plant imports, it was short-lived, virtually fading away by late spring. Perhaps the argument was finally resolved at the Central Work Conference in April 1971, although there is no evidence that economic matters loomed large at this meeting.[15] The difficulty in assessing the actual motive in these commentaries lies in their stress on local initiative in adapting foreign technology to Chinese needs. A campaign urging innovation and self-reliance began the previous winter but accelerated in March 1971. Thereafter, the emphasis shifted away from disparaging foreign techniques in favor of praising Chinese talents.

The only exception to this pattern came in September. A major JMJP article attacked alleged failures at the Tungfeng mine, attributing them to "leading personnel and designers" who were infected with "Liu's poison."[16] Because "they thought that as long as they had things 'large, foreign, and complete,' they would be technically 'advanced,'" therefore

> complete sets of large and foreign equipment were used
> in designs everywhere from the supply of air to rock
> cutting and lifting in vertical shafts to transportation in
> horizontal tunnels. At that time, some of the equipment
> was not yet manufactured domestically, some was still

being studied or tested and some could be found only in
foreign technical literature. They had a blind yearning
for "foreign" technology and wanted to copy things foreign regardless of whether they were useful or feasible.
Such disregard for objective conditions, worship of
things foreign and reliance on foreign countries for the
introduction of new technology were bound to divorce
them from reality.

Even here, however, the stress was less on the actual deficiencies of
foreign equipment than on the need to apply it correctly under the conditions prevailing in China.

Except for a brief spurt of relevant items in early January 1972,
little attention was given to the shortcomings of foreign technology for
the rest of that year and the next. Yet this was the most important
period for the allocation of authority to investigate sources, compare
equipment, negotiate details, and ultimately sign contracts. If any
opposition existed to this unprecedented degree of dependence on the
noncommunist world, it was publicly silent. Virtually no criticism,
direct or indirect, appeared in Chinese media.

1974-76

Not until 1974 did the first serious attack on whole plant imports
occur, foreshadowing the more explicit and extensive campaign of
1975-76. The timing is curious. By 1974 the import program had
already peaked, exceeding $1.2 billion for contracts concluded the pre-
vious year. The context for the new criticism included both economic
and political factors. In addition to the inflation-recession consequences
of the oil embargo, Chinese domestic politics were enlivened by the
return of Teng Hsiao-p'ing to prominence after his disappearance and
denunciation in 1966-68.

The basic themes of the campaign were laid out by Red Flag in
its first issue of the new year. The title encapsulated them, "Persist
in the Principle of Maintaining Independence and Keeping the Initiative
in Our Own Hands and Relying On Our Own Efforts in Achieving Regeneration."[17] After a lengthy diatribe against foreign equipment, the
author warned, "We cannot pin hope on others, still less can we pin
hope on large-scale importation of techniques and equipment from capitalist countries. . . . To develop industry by the importation of foreign
techniques and equipment not only is not a shortcut but is a tortuous,
evil path."

The author protected himself against appearing to attack extant policy by asserting, "We do not reject study of the advanced experiences of foreign countries. We have all along opposed the idea of great-nation chauvinism. . . . It is necessary to appropriately bring in advanced techniques and advanced equipment from foreign countries." However, he immediately reverted to his main theme: " . . . under no circumstances must we have blind faith in foreign things. . . . The fact that a small number of comrades in our ranks show blind faith in 'foreign equipment' and 'foreign techniques' is because they have not solidly established the viewpoint that 'the masses are true heroes.' . . . They do not understand that backward equipment in the hands of the advanced worker masses may be turned into advanced things and that advanced equipment in capitalist countries may not be put to maximum use."

Two months elapsed before the next attack but JMJP gave it full play in late March, now linking the foreign technology issue to the anti-Confucius campaign which had begun the previous fall. The indictment was strongly put: "Liu Shao-ch'i, Lin Piao and other ringleaders of the revisionist line like them revered Confucius, worshipped foreign things, trumpeted the slavish comprador philosophy and the mentality of trailing behind at a snail's pace and opposed Chairman Mao's correct line. This is a struggle between the proletariat and the bourgeoisie, between Marxism and revisionism, and between the socialist road and the capitalist road."[18]

The author pointedly recalled, "Shortly after the founding of new China, had not U.S. imperialism imposed an economic blockade on our country in a vain attempt to strangle the socialist new China? When our country was hit by serious natural disasters, had not Soviet revisionist imperialism betrayed us, withdrawn its specialists, and torn up contracts in a vain attempt to strangle us economically and force us to stay in line?" As for the policy of independence and self-reliance, "it will not do just to regard the implementation of this policy as an economic question and confine discussion to the matter at issue."

This political note won amplification in subsequent paragraphs which attacked Liu and Lin at length as having "worshipped Confucius and foreign things." Furthermore, the battle was not over. Although these past "renegades" had fallen, "it is necessary to see that the struggle is still continuing. The pernicious influence of the counter-revolutionary revisionist line of Lin Piao has still not been eliminated. The erroneous notion of blind faith in the 'advanced technology' of foreign countries still exists among some of the comrades. Could it be that we could not create the equipment and technique ourselves and could only rely on foreign countries?"

Consistent with the radicals' priority of emphasis which put politics over economics, the criticism was not couched in economic terms, despite the fact that throughout this period the twin threats of global inflation and recession loomed ever larger on the horizon. The negative implications for China's trade balance could not be missed. Yet this harsh fact of life was nowhere addressed in the many articles which followed these two major essays in attacking dependence on foreign technology and importation of advanced equipment. Instead, the earlier terminology of 1971 was given new meaning in the context of the anti-Confucius campaign which by this time served as a surrogate for attacking Chou En-lai. The criticism of foreign trade became a purely political weapon, couched in nativistic, implicitly xenophobic language but aimed more at domestic than foreign targets.

Intermittent lip service was given to "useful experiences of other countries" and "making foreign things serve China." Inevitably, however, these were passing remarks in an article overwhelmingly critical of foreign equipment and ways. The bulk of the articles in 1974 tread somewhat lightly by comparison with the later, more virulent attacks of 1975-76. Nonetheless, the juxtaposition of "self-reliance" versus "worshipping foreign things" clearly made the issue one of good versus evil, with obvious implications for anyone who took the latter course.

A different approach used historical analogy in a seemingly scholarly essay on "Worshipping Confucius and Reading the Classics, and Worshipping Things Foreign and Betraying the Country," in Red Flag of August 1974. After describing the activities of Tseng Kuo-fan, Yüan Shih-k'ai, and Chiang Kai-shek which purportedly exemplified the activities cited in the title, Li Hung-chang "served as a negative example, showing how an admirer of foreign things became a traitor." The characterization was a thinly disguised attack on Chou En-lai.

> He once shamelessly announced that "it is right and
> proper to be fond of talking about foreign affairs."
> Indeed, foreign affairs became the talk of the town.
> An expert on fawning on foreigners, he not only
> admired "the good of all other countries" but also
> begged for foreign capital economically. Equipment,
> raw materials, and technology were imported as
> "gifts" from the foreign imperialists, and foreign

66

experts were hired to run factories. In short,
everything became "modernized."[19]

A series of articles in the Shanghai theoretical journal, Study and Criticism (Hsüeh-hsi yu P'i P'an), appeared throughout 1974, ostensibly by workers in various factories. These invariably cited examples of past experience with Japanese, Soviet, or unidentified "foreign" technology which proved dangerous, uneconomic, or totally useless. The examples had sufficient specificity and technical detail as to appear authentic so far as lay readers were concerned.[20]

Articles in Red Flag, Study and Criticism, JMJP, and NCNA kept the issue alive throughout the year. Perhaps this was in response to mounting evidence of reliance on whole plants and foreign technology manifested by the presence of French, German, and Japanese advisors in increasing numbers at widely scattered points throughout China. In addition, it may have represented a determined effort to influence decisions prior to the Fourth National People's Congress (NPC) scheduled for January 1975. As the first such meeting since the Cultural Revolution, this gathering would legitimize policies adopted in the past and also chart the next Five Year Plan.

Against this background, KMJP carried an unusually long article on 6 January 1975. Cast in the now familiar form of historical analogy, it not only incorporated much of the Li Hung-chang material quoted above, but also focused on Chang Chih-tung as an example of "slavish comprador philosophy." As "the bureaucrat handling foreign affairs at the end of the Ch'ing Dynasty who worshipped things foreign and fawned on foreign powers," this article appeared to be directed against Teng Hsiao-p'ing, whose increasing prominence substituted for the ailing Chou. Stripped of its excessive historical detail, the essay was a direct critique of existing practices.

The author cited three factors to explain Chang's alleged failure in relying on foreign sources for technology:

> First, he depended on capitalism for capital. The
> majority of mines and factories he ran were financed
> with foreign debts. . . . Next, he relied on foreigners
> for technical knowledge and manpower. When start-
> ing each engineering project, he invariably made
> greater use of foreign artisans ranging from mineral
> prospecting, drawing, installation of machinery to

the construction of factory premises. Without
exception, well-known foreign specialists were
put in charge of work at all plants for refining
steel. . . . Third, complete sets of equipment
and supplies, ranging from major items such as
mining equipment and steel refining furnaces to
minor items such as sleepers, bricks, and
screws had to be imported from abroad.[21]

Among the numerous examples of Chang's erroneous policy which
had contemporary relevance, some of the most pointed remarks attacked
his attempt to develop an iron and steel industry on the basis of foreign
advisors and technology. This was of particular interest in view of
agreements concluded in the spring of 1974 for a $430 million steel
complex to be constructed in Wuhan involving more than two hundred
German and Japanese technicians. Another $100 million in associated
contracts were signed later that year. Production was to begin by 1977
at a cold rolling mill with a yearly capacity of 1.1 million metric tons,
a hot strip mill rated for 3 million metric tons, and a silicon plate mill
scheduled for 70 thousand metric tons yearly.

This extension of attack by analogy from individual policy makers
to specific projects was repeated in JMJP on 7 March 1975. The NPC
had endorsed Chou's call for catching up with advanced countries by
the year 2000 in the fields of science, industry, agriculture, and defense so as to create a "strong modern socialist economy." Neverthe-
less, the antiforeign campaign resumed after a brief hiatus. This
article attacked Liu and Lin for having ostensibly hampered the chemi-
cal fertilizer industry because of "blind faith in foreign equipment and
the worship of foreign dogma." The example cited was not fortuitous.
In 1973-74, contracts for nearly $370 million worth of chemical ferti-
lizer plants were signed, mainly with American and French companies
but also with Japanese, Dutch, and Danish firms. The foreign technicians were already on site when the article appeared but this apparently
did not inhibit its publication.

Another approach to foreign technology came under attack in the
June issue of Red Flag. With reference to the practice of licensing,
the article declared:

At the very mention of the manufacture of marine
diesel engines, some people would want to buy a
license, thinking that "buying a license is the sane

thing to do; developing it by ourselves is risky."
This is wrong. One year we intended to sign a
license agreement from a foreign capitalist.
According to this agreement, we would have to
pay a substantial amount of foreign exchange at
the beginning. After that, we would have to pay
a certain license fee for each engine made.
Besides, we would have to report to them twice
a year about our production plans and operations.
They would have the right to come to our shipyard for inspection. If disputes arose, these
would have to be subject to "arbitration" by third
countries. And so on and so forth.

. . . The workers said: to develop China's shipbuilding industry faster, we endorse buying some
licenses and importing some advanced technology
under the principle of equality and mutual benefit.
But if we have to accept such harsh conditions,
would this mean we allow foreign capitalists to
control the fate of our shipbuilding industry? We
can't buy such licenses ![22]

In October 1975, Liang Hsiao, a pseudonym associated with the Chiang
Ch'ing faction, recapitulated the various analogies from the nineteenth
and twentieth centuries in Historical Research (Li-shih Yen-chiu) and
indicted the importation of foreign technology on three points:

Politically "wholesale Westernization" meant
loss of sovereignty and national humiliation,
total sell-out of China's independence and self-
determination. . . . Ideologically "wholesale
Westernization" was meant to praise what is
foreign and belittle what is Chinese and propa-
gate national nihilism in order to undermine
the national consciousness of the Chinese
spirit. . . . Economically "wholesale Westernization" was aimed at spreading blind faith in
the Western capitalist material civilization so
as to turn the Chinese economy into a complete
appendage of imperialism.[23]

Although ostensibly pegged to the "Yang Wu" movement which espoused
"Chinese learning as the substance, Western learning as the function,"

the argument was traced through Hu Shih, Liu, and Lin to the present; "so deep-rooted has this reactionary philosophy been and so extensively has its poison spread that its influence is still felt today. Therefore it is still of practical significance to criticize the slavish comprador philosophy." This frank appeal to nativistic and xenophobic impulses revealed the basic political thrust of opposition to foreign technology and the deemphasis of economic factors.

The death of Chou En-lai in January 1976 was immediately followed by the disappearance of Teng and his replacement as acting premier by Hua Kuo-feng. The subsequent maneuvers which resulted in the Tienanmen riot of April and the formal naming of Hua as premier took the wraps off the anti-Teng campaign and also added a new indictment against the foreign trade program. Teng now was charged with bartering away China's natural resources in order to buy foreign technology. Although Red Flag authoritatively initiated this aspect of the anti-Teng movement in April, a particularly detailed indictment appeared in KMJP the same month. Speaking of Teng, it claimed:

> He again and again advocated relying on exports
> to secure imports for the development of industry
> and made an exaggerated description of the tech-
> nology and equipment introduced from other
> countries. He vociferously cried that it was
> necessary "to trade for the latest and best equip-
> ment of other countries" with our products. . . .
> As he saw it the four modernizations could be
> brought about through "trade." . . . He glibly
> expresses his desire for bartering exports for
> imports and even calls for relying on foreign
> technology, foreign equipment and foreign experts
> to exploit our national resources, thus assigning
> our mining rights to other people. What will be
> the consequences if this road is followed?[24]

The new stress on China's "national resources" took on added importance in the context of intermittent Sino-Japanese negotiations over a long-term agreement for Chinese oil. The sale of oil would offset China's heavy dependence on Japanese steel in addition to covering the large commitments for whole plants and machinery. Furthermore, American oil firms had in earlier months probed for PRC interest in offshore drilling equipment which could tap suspected reserves of staggering magnitude believed to lie in the continental shelf extending from the mainland to Korea, Japan, and Taiwan.

JMJP addressed the offshore oil problem directly on 28 July 1976 with an eloquent defense of self-reliance in the manufacture of drilling equipment as opposed to Teng's "slavish comprador" dependence on foreign technology. Subsequent articles repeatedly attacked the exchange of "complete sets of modern equipment" for "our industrial and mineral products" as "selling out our national resources." Potentially, much more than oil was at stake. Preliminary discussion had also occurred with foreign traders concerning possible future deliveries of liquefied natural gas. More immediately, China's vast coal reserves could be of major importance were Japan and others to revert to this energy source in lieu of oil or natural fuel.

The attacks on Teng mounted in intensity, including inter alia allegations of his "worshipping foreigners and fawning on foreign powers." JMJP carried the bitter reminiscences of workers at the Huting Shipyard in Shanghai concerning a Soviet agreement in 1951 "to supply China with the principal equipment, drawings, data, and experts. However, by 1960 when the trial production work was at the crucial stage, the Soviet revisionist renegade clique perfidiously and unscrupulously tore up the contracts and recalled their experts."[25] The workers cited Teng's celebrated statement concerning the worth of a cat that catches mice, whether white or black, declaring, "The inevitable outcome would be the unlimited import of what is needed at home. If this is allowed to go on, would not China once again sink to become an imperialist or social-imperialist satellite, and be trampled underfoot and carried up once again by imperialism?"

The Debate Ends: Retrospect and Conclusion

On 5 October 1976, JMJP fired the final salvoes from the opposition, echoing the charge that Teng advocated seeking help from the "Western lords," importing foreign technology, and relying on complete sets of foreign equipment with payment from China in mineral products and national resources. He allegedly regarded his critics as suffering from "sheer arrogance" and "isolationism." Within a week, Chiang Ch'ing and her associates--the Gang of Four--disappeared beneath a tidal wave of denunciation exceeding in its public demonstrations and apparent jubilation anything since the mammoth Red Guard rallies of 1966. Among the many accusations levelled at them was the charge that they had obstructed foreign trade and opposed imports of technology.

In early November high Chinese officials stressed renewed interest in the importation of plants and machinery for petrochemicals, oil exploitation, steelworks, and electrical production. While acknowledging that "foreign currency problems" existed, they alluded to their possession of "oil and coal" as "important."[26]

On 10 November, KMJP began what was to become a wholesale indictment of the Gang with respect to foreign trade. Declaring "it is now about time to strip off their masks," the "mass criticism group of the Ministry of Coal Industry" utilized the past polemics as evidence that "they have indiscriminately referred to the practice of planned and selective procurement of foreign technology as 'servility to things foreign,' 'trailing behind others at a snail's pace,' 'worshipping things foreign and fawning upon foreigners,' 'capitulationism and national betrayal,' 'modern compradorism' and so forth."[27] The Gang stood accused of "tampering with and citing out of context Chairman Mao's directives." Moreover, in turning the table, the writers used the identical polemics to indict the Gang for being "out-and-out foreigner worshippers and honest-to-goodness slavish compradors," having "kowtowed to their foreign masters [and] committed themselves completely to capitulationism and national betrayal."

These charges were elaborated upon somewhat in JMJP and local radio broadcasts during December. However, a lengthy NCNA dispatch of 13 January 1977 made detailed allegations concerning the Gang's obstruction of foreign trade which went far beyond anything previously suspected, much less known. Allowing for rhetorical flourishes and polemical exaggeration, the article nonetheless justifies attention as highly plausible in light of our earlier analysis.

Explicitly addressing events in 1976, the article claimed that in March, "at a meeting without authorization [and] behind the backs of Chairman Mao and the Central Committee," Chiang Ch'ing charged that oil "had been given to foreign countries and sold to those big capitalists" by "agents of international capitalists and comprador bourgeoisie."[28] Further attacks allegedly occurred at three meetings "convened by the central authorities from March to June." Wang Hung-wen purportedly targetted the foreign trade departments while Chang Ch'un-ch'iao hit the Politburo as "bourgeoisie and comprador bourgeoisie."

Chang and Wang "sent people by plane from Shanghai to the Ministry of Foreign Trade to . . . slander the ministry as 'practicing capitulationism and national betrayal.'" Chang and Yao "also used the mass media . . . to publish numerous sinister articles and energetically create counterrevolutionary public opinion." Moreover, the Gang placed "their people in the Ministry of Foreign Trade, foreign trade departments in a number of localities, and the Canton trade fair" who "wrote and gathered sinister materials and then sent them to Yao Wen-yuan for his personal copying."[29] These materials were then sent "to the representatives of various provinces and municipalities and various departments and ministries under the central authorities attending a conference."

Beyond these communications and organization activities, according to NCNA, the Gang worked to interfere with the export of oil:

> In 1976 alone, that sworn follower of the "gang of four"
> in Liaoning had willfully increased the number of oil-
> consuming units by more than a hundred. Shanghai's
> crude oil consumption for 1976 exceeded the plan by
> 1 million tons. . . . Under the pretext of "protecting
> Shanghai" it forced the central department concerned
> to give its approval to intercept crude oil at Shanghai
> harbor destined for the tankers at Wusungkou . . . and
> seized a total of 200,000 tons of crude oil. . . . Not
> only this, but as a result of the interference and dis-
> ruption of the "gang of four" oil exports were also
> affected. This harmed our country's credibility and
> had negative effects both politically and economically.

The "importation of whole sets of equipment" was criticized by Chang: "Too many major items have been imported. They have been clustered together." Actually, according to the article, the Gang knew that "the import of all these entire sets of equipment was approved by Chairman Mao" and "they themselves had signed their names to these reports and the locations of some of the plants had been selected by them." Chang's criticism is the closest to an economic argument to be found in published materials attributable to the opposition. Perhaps he also raised the unfavorable trade balance and the uncertainties of world market conditions, positions which could not have been as easily rebutted. If so, their post hoc suppression is understandable. Whatever may have been the private lines of debate, however, the public record supports the proposition that in 1976, politics, not economics, suspended trading activity in whole plant imports.

To recapitulate, the strictures against foreign technology in 1971 emerged in the campaign for indigenous technical innovation and do not seem to have carried additional connotations of an attack on forth-coming policy. If they were so intended they had no effect as evidenced by the surge of contracts signed in 1973-74. The first clear attack on the importation of whole plants did not occur until the January 1974 Red Flag article, reiterated in JMJP of 22 March 1974. Yet, the peak period of agreements totalling $1.2 billion had already occurred in 1973. Nor can the cutback to $850 million in 1974 and $364 million in 1975 be clearly attributed to political factors. These are impressive amounts in themselves. Moreover, these reductions logically followed from the limits on payment obligations that are a result of China's refusal to accept long-term loans and constraints on her export earnings, coupled with the immediate combination of inflation and recession in the international economy.

Only in 1976 did the situation develop so as to force a suspension of contract activity because of domestic politics. As early as August 1974, historical allegory had thinly screened the shift from a general broadside against foreign imports and dependence to an attack on Chou En-lai. However, the ascendancy of the Chou-Teng faction in the National People's Congress of January 1975 stilled the opposition for three months, after which time the attack focused on specific foreign technology dependent programs such as iron and steel.

During mid-1975, the Gang gradually increased its ideological pressure. As Chou's health steadily failed, the opposition became more programmatic in building its case against Teng. But only after Chou's death did the accusers name Teng. They also moved into the open by attacking the export of oil to support their charge of "national betrayal." Even so, discussions with foreign sources of whole plants and equipment worth nearly $200 million occurred in early 1976. However, after the April riots and final replacement of Teng by Hua, manifest tension and uncertainty among Chinese negotiators finally brought these discussions to a halt by midyear.

In sum, the importation of whole plants served the Gang as a whipping boy to be used as domestic politics permitted. But domestic politics proved to be a severe constraint, at times silencing the opposition completely and often forcing it to attack obliquely. The period between the deaths of Chou and Mao was short-lived. The speed with which Chinese officials reaffirmed their interest in foreign technology after Mao's death and the demise of the Gang underscored the degree to which domestic politics had uniquely affected recent economic behavior. China's ability to fund imports had not improved between April and October 1976. On the contrary, production had plummeted from political disruption and earthquakes. Yet, foreign audiences now were reassured that imports would again be increased and domestic audiences were thereafter informed that the Gang had obstructed and sabotaged this program in 1976.

While the political atmosphere changed markedly in 1976, first unfavorably and then favorably so far as whole plant imports were concerned, the practical consequences were less dramatically evident. Economic and technical constraints limited the level of contracts that could be signed. One year after the Gang had disappeared, no great surge to the 1973-74 levels had occurred. Nor had any change occurred in the five year limit on deferred payment. However, it seemed certain the post-Mao regime would shortly increase the importation of foreign technology and whole plants to maintain the momentum of modernization and growth approved at the Fourth National People's Congress in January 1975 and reinstated at Premier Hua Kuo-feng's address to the Fifth NPC in February 1978. If politics prevailed over economics in the short run, in the long run economics seemed certain to prevail.

Implications

The foregoing analysis bears on the prospects for China's importation of whole plants and advanced technology in several respects. First, it suggests that so long as the preponderance of political power is in the hands of individuals and groups whose outlook is favorable to rapid modernization and technological advance, major weight will be given to foreign sources of technology. The elimination of Chiang Ch'ing together with the elevation of Teng Hsiao-p'ing assures that this outlook will prevail for at least the next several years.

Secondly, the recurring appearance of nativistic and xenophobic themes in the public media, either with or without actual policy relevance for foreign trade, indicates the political volatility of dependence on whole plant imports. The bitter pre-1949 experience as well as that of the "lean to one side" period of 1949-60 provides ample material for political exploitation in this regard. This material may be used opportunistically by opposing factions with greater or lesser effect on actual trade, depending upon the balance of contending coalitions at the time. It cannot be assumed in advance that groups favorable to imports will consistently prevail or that economic rationality will necessarily determine policy.

Thirdly, to the extent that imports are funded by the export of natural resources, such as oil, they will be particularly vulnerable to this type of attack. In particular, joint ownership proposals, consortium arrangements, or other forms of mixed enterprise that involve foreign capital and management require a supremely self-confident and secure leadership, whether individual or collective. Regardless of the economic inducements that might be offered by outside sources of investment and equipment, the political liability of being cast in the role of "slavish comprador" or "practicing capitulationism and national betrayal" will remain for some time to come, at least into the 1980s.

Lastly, the continuing justification of foreign trade as "serving China's needs" and aiming at eventual "self-reliance" indicates a basic thrust of policy that is more than a rhetorical defense against accusations of "worshipping foreign things." It would be hazardous to project consistent export-import patterns on the basis of present policy statements. In addition to the economic problems of absorption and payment, the political sense of inferiority associated with reliance on foreign technology and advice rubs against Chinese self-esteem, heightened by the post-1949 claim to having "stood up." This mitigates against the relaxed acceptance of interdependence as an inevitable component of modernization and industrialization. Internal tensions may increase as foreign trade expands and impose intermittent cutbacks, accompanied by strictures against such trade similar to those examined above.

All this suggests that while the Gang of Four is politically dead, its criticisms cannot be wholly buried. The program of whole plant imports and dependence on foreign technology will remain liable to the vicissitudes of domestic politics. It will also be affected by the behavior of foreign traders and technicians. The cultural and experiential gulf which separates Chinese from their Western counterparts poses a challenge in communication during both the negotiation of a contract and its implementation. The ideological gulf heightens this problem. In addition to the obvious counterpoint between communism and capitalism, the basic societal values of daily living differentiate post-1949 China from most of its trading partners. Nor will the embourgeoisement which can already be glimpsed in the elite and in the few cosmopolitan cities of Peking, Shanghai, and Canton suddenly sweep over the vast countryside so as to narrow these points of separation and difference.

In sum, the foreign trader and technician enters China against a basic prejudice born out of past experience and recent politics. The prospect for steadily enlarging China's dependence upon and involvement with a world economy is limited by the need to build a far firmer foundation of mutual interest, sensitivity, and trust than has existed to date. To the extent that this foundation depends upon foreign behavior, it can be facilitated through careful, conscious effort. To the extent that this remains subject to domestic politics, however, the outcome lies largely in Chinese hands.

APPENDIX A

CHINA: CONTRACTS FOR WHOLE PLANT IMPORTS

Nation/Firm	Type	Value (Million US $)	Contract Signed	Completion	Comment
1973 Contracts		1,259			
Japan		461			
Toyo Engineering	Ethylene and butadiene	50	Feb 73	1978	Japan Ex-Im/Commercial bank financing
Mitsubishi	Ethylene and poval	34	Feb 73	N.A.	Japan Ex-Im/Commercial bank financing
Asahi Chemical	Acrylonitrile monomer	30	Mar 73	N.A.	Japan Ex-Im/Commercial bank financing
Kuraray	Vinyl acetate and poval	26	Mar 73	1976	Japan Ex-Im/Commercial bank financing
Toyo Engineering and Mitsui Toatsu	Urea and ammonia	42	Apr 73	N.A.	Japan Ex-Im/Commercial bank financing
Toray and Mitsui Ship-building	Polyester chips	50	May 73	1976	Japan Ex-Im/Commercial bank financing
Sumitomo	Benzene, toluene, xylene	5	May 73	N.A.	Cash deal
Mitsubishi	Polyethylene, low pressure	22	Jul 73	1975	Japan Ex-Im/Commercial bank financing
Sumitomo	Polyethylen, high pressure	47	Aug 73	1976	Japan Ex-Im/Commercial bank financing
Hitachi Ltd.	Two thermal electric power plants	72	Sep 73	1975	Japan Ex-Im/Commercial bank financing
Toyo Engineering and Mitsui Toatsu	Urea and ammonia	43	Sep 73	N.A.	Japan Ex-Im/Commercial bank financing

Appendix A--continued

Nation/Firm	Type	Value (Million US $)	Contract Signed	Completion	Comment
Mitsui Petrochemical and Mitsui Shipbuilding	Polypropylene	25	Oct 73	1976	Japan Ex-Im/Commercial bank financing
NISSO Petrochemical	Ethylene glycol	15	Dec 73	1977	Japan Ex-Im/Commercial bank financing
France		400			
Alsthom	Hydroelectric turbines (2)	10	Feb 73	N.A.	
Speichem	Vinyl acetate and methanol	90	May 73	1976	Consortium involving firms in France. West Germany, and the United Kingdom
Technip and Speichem	Petrochemical complex	300	Sep 73	N.A.	French-led consortium probably involving other firms in Western Europe
United States		205			
M.W. Kellogg	Ammonia plants (3)	75	Mar 73	1976	Probable feedstock plants for the Dutch urea plants
M.W. Kellogg	Ammonia plants (5)	130	Nov 73	1976-77	Probably progress payments; will provide feedstock for five Dutch urea plants
Netherlands		89			
Kellogg Continental	Urea plants (3)	34	Feb 73	1976	Subsidiary of M.W. Kellogg
Kellogg Continental	Urea plants (5)	55	Sep 73	1977	Subsidiary of M.W. Kellogg

West Germany Friedrich Uhde and Hoechst	Acetaldehyde	4 4	Jul 73	N.A.	
United Kingdom Technicolor Ltd.	Motion picture processing plant	8 8	Jul 73	N.A.	
Italy G.I.E.	Electric thermal power-plants (2)	79 79	Nov 73	N.A.	Five-year financing
Denmark Haldor Topsoe	Ammonia catalyst	13 13	Dec 73	N.A.	
1974 Contracts		831 348			
Japan Teijin	Polyester spinning	16	Jan 74	N.A.	Japan Ex-Im/Commercial financing
Toho Titanium	Polypropylene catalyst	5	Jan 74	N.A.	Catalyst for Mitsui polypropylene plant
Kuraray	Polyvinyl alcohol	19	Feb 74	1976	Japan Ex-Im/Commercial bank financing
NISSO Petrochemical	Synthetic fiber	14	Mar 74	1976	
Nippon Steel & Hitachi	Hot strip rolling mill and silicon steel plate	229	Jun 74	1977	Demag supplying other part of the complex
Nippon Steel	Ancillary equipment for steel mill	65	Oct 74	1977	Equipment for the hot strip mill
West Germany Uhde	Vinyl chloride monomer	296 19	Jan 74	1976	

Appendix A--continued

Nation/Firm	Type	Value (Million US $)	Contract Signed	Completion	Comment
West Germany, cont.					
Demag	Cold rolling mill	200	Mar 74	1977	Consortium of European firms led by Demag. Progress payment.
Uhde	Polyethylene	15	Mar 74	1976	
Demag	Continuous casting mill	57	Aug 74	1977	Progress payment. Part of steel complex purchased from Japan and Germany
Brown Boveri	Electrical substations	5	Aug 74	1977	
France		171			
Heurtey	Ammonia and urea complex (2)	120	Feb 74	1977	Five-year credit financing
Electromechanique	Thermal electric powerplant	41	Apr 74	1976	
Rhone Poulenc	Nylon spinning	10	Aug 74	1977	Progress payments
Italy		16			
SNAM Progetti	Polypropylene	16	Jan 74	N.A.	Progress payments

APPENDIX B

CHINA: CONTRACTS FOR WHOLE PLANT IMPORTS

Nation/Firm	Type	Value (Million US $)	Contract Signed	Completion	Comment
1975 Contracts		364			
Japan					
Nippon Seiko	Spherical bearings	3	Apr 75	1976	Progress payments
Koyo Seiko	Cylindrical bearings	8	Apr 75	1976	Progress payments
Ibigawa	Laminated board	1	Jul 75	N.A.	
Ataka	Air separation	11	Nov 75	1977	Progress payments; 35,000 m³/hr capacity
Mitsubishi	Friction materials	15	Dec 75	N.A.	
West Germany		90			
Linde	Benzene	20	Jul 75	N.A.	
Krupp	Dimethyltherephthalate	50	Dec 75	N.A.	Progress payments; 90,000 t/yr capacity
Uhde	Ethanol	20	Dec 75	N.A.	100,000 MT/yr capacity
United Kingdom		200			
Rolls Royce	Jet engine plant	200	Dec 75	1980	50 jet engines plus manufacturing facility and testing equipment
Italy		36			
Mechaniche Moderne	Detergent	1	Sep 75	N.A.	Progress payments
Eurotechnica	Detergent alkalation	35	Oct 75	N.A.	Deferred payments

Appendix B--continued

Nation/Firm	Type	Value (Million US $)	Contract Signed	Completion	Comment
1976 Contracts		185			
Japan		146			
Japan Gasoline	Aromatics complex	36	Jan 76	N.A.	Japan Ex-Im Bank financing
Japan Synthetic Rubber	Styrene-butadiene rubber	27	Feb 76	N.A.	5-year Japan Ex-Im Bank financing; 240,000 MT/yr capacity
Kyokuto Boeki Kaisha	Hot scarfer	2	Mar 76	N.A.	Progress payments
Teijin	Polyester/polymer	40	Mar 76	N.A.	5-year Japan Ex-Im Bank financing; 80,000 MT/yr capacity
Nakajima Seiki	Wallpaper plant	1	Apr 76	N.A.	
Nippon Steel	Desulfurization plant	26	Jun 76	N.A.	
Mitsui	Cinder pelletizing	14	Aug 76	N.A.	
West Germany		31			
BASF	Diethylhexonol	24	Mar 76	N.A.	50,000 MT/yr capacity
Kraus Maffei	High reactive lime	7	Aug 76	N.A.	
Italy		8			
Nuovo Pignone	Centrifugal compressors technology	8	Jun 76	N.A.	
Finland		N.A.			
Tamglass	Automobile glass plant	N.A.	Jun 76	N.A.	

NOTES

1. Roy Grow, Politics of Industrial Development in China.

2. During 1975 foreign engineers in China were severely restricted in their freedom of movement within their immediate areas of activity and residence, so much so as to preclude virtually all contact with the local inhabitants except as necessitated by their work; interviews by the author.

3. Alexander Eckstein, Communist China's Economic Growth and Foreign Trade (New York: McGraw-Hill, 1966).

4. Central Intelligence Agency, Research Aid: People's Republic of China: Foreign Trade in Machinery and Equipment Since 1952 (Washington, D.C., 1975).

5. Information provided by the Department of State.

6. Jürgen Domes, China After the Cultural Revolution (Berkeley: University of California Press, 1977), chapter 5.

7. Kenneth Lieberthal, A Research Guide to Central Party and Government Meetings In China, 1949-1975 (White Plains, N.Y.: International Arts and Sciences Press, Inc., 1976).

8. This paragraph is drawn from information provided by the Department of State.

9. Central Intelligence Agency, China: International Trade, 1976-1977 (Washington, D.C., 1977).

10. Ibid.

11. Interviews by the author.

12. "Scientific Research Must Be Combined With Production Practice," JMJP, 6 January 1971, in SCMP, no. 4821-25, 18-22 January 1971.

13. Lieberthal, Research Guide, pp. 273-76.

14. "Design and Manufacture More and Better Mining Machines for Developing the Iron and Steel Industry," Revolutionary Mass Criticism Writing Group of First Ministry of Machine Building, JMJP, 1 March 1971, in SCMP, no. 4866, 26 March 1971.

15. Lieberthal, Research Guide, p. 276.

16. "Develop Revolution in Designing and Persevere in Building of Large Mines by Stages," Revolutionary Mass Criticism and Repudiation Team of Shansi Non-ferrous Metal Company, JMJP, 3 September 1971, in SCMP, no. 4977, 17 September 1971.

17. Wei Ping-k'uei, "Persist in the Principle of Maintaining Independence and Keeping the Initiative in Our Own Hands and Relying on Our Own Efforts in Achieving Regeneration," Red Flag, no. 1, 1 January 1974, in SPRCM, nos. 767-68, 21 January-4 February 1974.

18. Tien Chin-sung, "Adhere to the Policy of Independence and Self-reliance," JMJP, 22 March 1974, in SPRCP, no. 5584, 1 April 1974.

19. Ch'en Chin, "Worshipping Things Foreign and Betraying the Country," Red Flag, no. 8, 1 August 1974, in SPRCM, no. 787-88, 3 August-9 September 1974.

20. See for example Ch'en Ts'ai-ming, "Take Our Own Road of Developing New Technology," Study and Criticism, no. 8, 20 August 1974, in SPRCM, no. 789, 20 September 1974.

21. "The Bankruptcy of the Philosophy of Servility to Things Foreign as Viewed from the Failure of Chang Chih-tung in Handling Foreign Affairs," Kuang-ming Jih-pao, 6 January 1975, in SPRCP, no. 5780, 24 January 1975.

22. "Take the Tach'ing Road, Build a 'Railway on the Sea'," Red Flag, no. 6, 1 June 1975, in SPRCM, nos. 827-28, 30 June-7 July 1975.

23. Liang Hsiao, "The Yang Wu Movement and the Slavish Comprador Philosophy," Historical Research, no. 5, 20 October 1975, in SPRCM, no. 850, 16 December 1975.

24. Chin Feng, "Thoroughly Criticize the Slavish Comprador Philosophy Publicized by Teng Hsiao-p'ing," Kuang-ming Jih-pao,
21 April 1976, in SPRCP, no. 6086, 3 May 1976.

25. Jen-min Jih-pao, 14 June 1976, in SCMP, no. 6123, 25 June 1976.

26. Peking, Agence France Presse, 2, 4, and 5 November 1976, in
FBIS, 3, 5, and 8 November 1976.

27. Kuang-ming Jih-pao, 10 November 1976, in FBIS, 22 November 1976.

28. Peking NCNA, domestic service in Chinese, 13 January 1977, in
FBIS, 14 January 1977.

29. According to a well-placed informant, Chiang Ch'ing won access
to decisions on foreign trade by utilizing her legitimate role in
cultural affairs. She attended the advance showing of items scheduled for export through the Canton Trade Fair and criticized the
use of classical themes and imperial symbols which were no longer
permitted within China. She expanded from this point to be a more
general overseer of all foreign trade; confidential interview by the
author.

MICHIGAN PAPERS IN CHINESE STUDIES

No. 2. The Cultural Revolution: 1967 in Review, four essays by Michel Oksenberg, Carl Riskin, Robert Scalapino, and Ezra Vogel.

No. 3. Two Studies in Chinese Literature, by Li Chi and Dale Johnson.

No. 4. Early Communist China: Two Studies, by Ronald Suleski and Daniel Bays.

No. 5. The Chinese Economy, ca. 1870-1911, by Albert Feuerwerker.

No. 6. Chinese Paintings in Chinese Publications, 1956-1968: An Annotated Bibliography and an Index to the Paintings, by E. J. Laing.

No. 7. The Treaty Ports and China's Modernization: What Went Wrong? by Rhoads Murphey.

No. 8. Two Twelfth Century Texts on Chinese Painting, by Robert J. Maeda.

No. 9. The Economy of Communist China, 1949-1969, by Chu-yuan Cheng.

No. 10. Educated Youth and the Cultural Revolution in China, by Martin Singer.

No. 11. Premodern China: A Bibliographical Introduction, by Chun-shu Chang.

No. 12. Two Studies on Ming History, by Charles O. Hucker.

No. 13. Nineteenth Century China: Five Imperialist Perspectives, selected by Dilip Basu, edited by Rhoads Murphey.

No. 14. Modern China, 1840-1972: An Introduction to Sources and Research Aids, by Andrew J. Nathan.

No. 15. Women in China: Studies in Social Change and Feminism, edited by Marilyn B. Young.

No. 16. An Annotated Bibliography of Chinese Painting Catalogues and Related Texts, by Hin-cheung Lovell.

No. 17. China's Allocation of Fixed Capital Investment, 1952-1957, by Chu-yuan Cheng.

No. 18. Health, Conflict, and the Chinese Political System, by David M. Lampton.

No. 19. Chinese and Japanese Music-Dramas, edited by J. I. Crump and William P. Malm.

MICHIGAN ABSTRACTS OF CHINESE AND
JAPANESE WORKS ON CHINESE HISTORY

No. 1. The Ming Tribute Grain System, by Hoshi Ayao, translated by Mark Elvin.

No. 2. Commerce and Society in Sung China, by Shiba Yoshinobu, translated by Mark Elvin.

No. 3. Transport in Transition: The Evolution of Traditional Shipping in China, translations by Andrew Watson.

No. 4. Japanese Perspectives on China's Early Modernization: A Bibliographical Survey, by K. H. Kim.

No. 5. The Silk Industry in Ch'ing China, by Shih Min-hsiung, translated by E-tu Zen Sun.

NONSERIES PUBLICATION

Index to the "Chan-kuo Ts'e," by Sharon Fidler and J. I. Crump. A companion volume to the Chan-kuo Ts'e, translated by J. I. Crump (Oxford: Clarendon Press, 1970).

Michigan Papers and Abstracts available from:

Center for Chinese Studies
The University of Michigan
Lane Hall (Publications)
Ann Arbor, MI 48109 USA

Prepaid Orders Only
write for complete price listing

www.ingramcontent.com/pod-product-compliance
Lightning Source LLC
Chambersburg PA
CBHW022124280326
41933CB00007B/530